Trading the China Market with American Depository Receipts

Founded in 1807, John Wiley & Sons is the oldest independent publishing company in the United States. With offices in North America, Europe, Australia and Asia, Wiley is globally committed to developing and marketing print and electronic products and services for our customers' professional and personal knowledge and understanding.

The Wiley Trading series features books by traders who have survived the market's ever changing temperament and have prospered—some by reinventing systems, others by getting back to basics. Whether a novice trader, professional or somewhere in-between, these books will provide the advice and strategies needed to prosper today and well into the future.

For a list of available titles, visit our website at www.WileyFinance.com.

Trading the China Market with American Depository Receipts

How to Play Greater China with a Winning Edge

ALAN VOON

WILEY

John Wiley & Sons Singapore Pte. Ltd.

Other Wiley Editorial Offices

John Wiley & Sons, 111 River Street, Hoboken, NJ 07030, USA

John Wiley & Sons, The Atrium, Southern Gate, Chichester, West Sussex, P019 8SQ, United
Kingdom

John Wiley & Sons (Canada) Ltd., 5353 Dundas Street West, Suite 400, Toronto, Ontario, M9B
6HB, Canada

John Wiley & Sons Australia Ltd., 42 McDougall Street, Milton, Queensland 4064, Australia

Wiley-VCH, Boschstrasse 12, D-69469 Weinheim, Germany

ISBN 978-1-11831602-3 (Cloth)
ISBN 978-1-11831603-0 (ePDF)
ISBN 978-1-11831604-7 (Mobi)
ISBN 978-1-11831605-4 (ePub)

Typeset in 10/12 pt, Century Std Book by MPS Limited, Chennai, India.

10 9 8 7 6 5 4 3 2 1

Contents

Preface

When I was at university, my finance professor kept saying that there was no free lunch in the stock market. Indeed, it is very difficult to find free lunches or risk-free profits, especially in today's well-connected global market place, where any new piece of information is immediately digested and reflected in market prices.

While the above statement is true to a large extent, there must be some way to get a free lunch, as I do not believe the market is completely efficient. Residing in a country where the capital market is not sufficiently well developed, I do find risk-free opportunities in the stock market and have been able to take advantage of such opportunities as they arose in the past.

As someone who treats the stock market as the love of his life, I strive to gain an edge in investing by exploring many non-mainstream investment approaches and utilizing various instruments to enhance return. I have since written two books on warrants and how to achieve better returns using such derivatives catering to the local market. But, I always wanted to write a book that had mass international appeal.

Through many months of research and real-life experience, I managed to discover a relatively risk-free trading strategy utilizing price-moving, after-market news in Asia to build a position in ADRs and/or their derivatives (where available) in the U.S. markets. When the news indeed moved the share price the next trading day in Asia, profits could then be realized when the U.S. market opened and the open position was closed. I truly believe this strategy can help investors and traders from all over the world to acquire some free lunches in the stock market.

Part One of this book begins with a case study of a company associated with the richest man of Chinese origin, and how I utilized after-hours market earnings announcements to trade the company's ADR listed in the United States, making money before the ADR prices reflected the earnings news.

I then go on to introduce ADRs in Chapter 2. Different types of ADRs are explained and also the mechanism of creating and canceling ADRs. To make it easier for you to start utilizing this strategy, I also present ten companies that you should keep an eye on to take advantage of possible price-moving news.

In Chapter 3, I offer where to look for possible price-moving news released in the after-hours Asia market. I also give a brief guide to how such news can be interpreted.

Chapter 4 is more about practical knowledge to start implementing the strategy. I also talk about what facilities the stockbroker must provide in order for traders to better implement such strategies.

After equipping you with information to give you a trading edge, I indicate that you must maximize such opportunities when available to enhance gain. Chapter 5 discusses when to introduce various derivatives to magnify trading gains.

Chapter 6 deals with the possible pitfalls of using this strategy and provides examples of when such a seemingly sure thing can sometimes go wrong.

Part Two comprises Chapters 7 to 10. In it, case studies illustrate how the strategies in Part One can be implemented when companies announce earnings surprises and shocks. I also point out that changes in government policies can have an impact on share price. Finally, some examples dealing with company specific news are illustrated.

I have been using the strategies in this book to make money with ADRs when opportunities arise following significant price-moving news released after Asian markets close. After reading this book, I am sure many traders will be able to join me in making some easy money from the stock market.

Acknowledgments

I would like to express my deepest gratitude to the friends and business associates who helped me out in developing this book. I am especially grateful to Paul Lau and Kathy Fong who spent time writing the appendix and editing some of my work.

I want to express my deep appreciation to Caitlin Duffy from Interactive Brokers who assisted me in looking for source materials and even doing some editing work. I also wish to thank Vivien Wang from Huatai Securities Group and my assistant Denken Tan who helped me to identify some examples for case studies in this book.

Nick Wallwork from John Wiley & Sons has been instrumental in making this book a reality. I am indebted to him for helping me to share my work with a worldwide audience. I'd also like to thank Emilie Herman and Jennifer MacDonald in the editing of the book.

Last, but not least, I wish to thank my parents and family members who have supported me in achieving my goal to excel in investing and to gain international recognition in my field of expertise.

PART I

An Introduction to American Depository Receipts

CHAPTER 1

How I Discovered Making Money in China with American Depository Receipts (ADRs)

The date was August 5, 2010; the Asian stock markets had already closed and it was early in the morning in North America. Hutchison Whampoa Limited, the flagship company of Li Ka-Shing, the richest man of Chinese origin and the eleventh richest man in the world with an estimated wealth of US$22 billion, had just released its latest interim results ended June 30, 2010. Records on the Hong Kong Stock Exchange indicated that the earnings report was released at 4:17 p.m. Hong Kong time.

A CASE STUDY

Hutchison Whampoa announced that it had achieved net profit (profit attributable to shareholders) of HK$6.45 billion for the six-month period ending June 30, 2010. That is a growth of 12 percent over net profit of HK$5.76 billion achieved during the same period in 2009. While a 12 percent growth in earnings may be viewed upon as mildly positive news for those not following the company closely, the investment community was actually expecting Hutchison Whampoa to record a decline in earnings. Analysts at that time had forecasted Hutchison Whampoa to only achieve

TABLE 1.1   Hutchison Whampoa Interim Results

HK$ Billion	Half-Year Ending 6/30/10	Half-Year Ending 6/30/09	Change
Revenue	152.9	141.0	8%
Net Profit	6.45	5.76	12%
EPS (HK$)	1.51	1.35	12%

TABLE 1.2   Hutchison Whampoa Limited ADR

DR Symbol	HUWHY
CUSIP	448415208
DR Exchange	OTC
DR ISIN	US4484152081
Ratio	1:2
Depository	Various (Unsponsored)
Effective Date	Jan 15, 1983
Underlying ISIN	HK0013000119
Underlying SEDOL	6448068
Underlying Symbol	0013. HK
Country	Hong Kong
Industry	General Industrial

Source: BNY Mellon (www.adrbnymellon.com).

a net profit of around HK$4.5 billion, representing a decline of more than 20 percent in earnings. See Table 1.1.

In the note accompanying the interim results, Hutchison Whampoa indicated that there was no profit on disposal of investments in the first half of 2010 while it did report such profit of some HK$4.7 billion in the first half of 2009. Had such disposal of investments profits been excluded, earnings in the first half of 2010 were actually 270 percent higher than in the first half of 2009.

So it was not merely a profit growth of 12 percent, but high triple-digit growth in operating profit. Analysts forecasted growth in operating profit but they obviously missed the big picture. When analysts miss big, the share price of Hutchison Whampoa is expected to soar upon resumption of trading the next day in Hong Kong where the company is listed.

Little known to most, Hutchison Whampoa is actually also traded in the U.S. stock market. The company actually never listed its shares in the United States but a few banks—including BNY Mellon, JP Morgan, and Citibank—issued Hutchison Whampoa American Depository Receipts (ADR). Hutchison Whampoa ADR is quoted under the symbol HUWHY over-the-counter at Pink OTC Markets or Pink Sheets. See Table 1.2.

TABLE 1.3	Price Range of Hutchison Whampoa Share Price and its ADR Equivalent Price Adjusted for ADR Ratio and Exchange Rate in HK$ on the Days before and after its Earnings Surprise

| | **Actual Underlying Share Price** | | | **Equivalent ADR Price (adjusted) ADR Price in Bracket (US$)** | | |
Date	High	Low	Close	High	Low	Close
08/04/2010	53.00	52.30	53.00	53.26(13.72)	52.79(13.60)	53.15(13.69)
08/05/2010	53.20	52.50	53.05	53.14(13.69)	52.40(13.50)	53.09(13.68)
08/06/2010	58.45	53.90	58.20	58.04(14.96)	56.80(14.64)	57.75(14.88)

On August 5, 2010, Hutchison Whampoa ADR or HUWHY traded between US$13.50 to US$13.69 (after adjusting for ADR ratio change and stock distribution carried out in June 2011. The ADR ratio was 1:5 before that in the United States). This is equivalent to HK$52.40 to HK$53.14 (based on the exchange rate of HK$7.7624 per US$ on that day). This is within the price range of the Hong Kong exchange-quoted Hutchison Whampoa underlying share of in between HK$52.50 to HK$53.20 on August 5, 2010, as indicated in Table 1.3.

Table 1.3 shows that the U.S. market traded Hutchison Whampoa ADR at a price on August 5, 2010, that did not reflect the expected price surge of Hutchison Whampoa on the next trading day. The ADR price typically tracks the underlying share price closely. Sometimes, the ADR may trade at a premium or discount to the equivalent price of the underlying share listed on the home market. However, such price discrepancies tend to be small due to the presence of arbitraging activities between the ADR and its underlying share. If the ADR trades at a big discount to the underlying share, an investor can always buy the ADR, get the depository bank to exchange the ADRs for the underlying ordinary shares held in custody, and then proceed to sell these shares in the home market for a profit.

As such, Hutchison Whampoa's share price in Hong Kong was expected to surge on August 6, 2010, when the shares resumed trading after digesting the earnings surprise. We could purchase Hutchison Whampoa ADR on August 5, 2010, between US$13.50 to US$13.69, before that happened.

On the next day (August 6) in Hong Kong, the Hutchison Whampoa share price reacted to the company's earnings, blowing past analysts' estimates and surging to close at HK$58.20, a gain of almost 10 percent of the previous day's closing price of HK$53.05.

As a result, Hutchison Whampoa ADR opened a gap up on August 6, 2010, at US$14.76 and closed the day at US$14.88, or a gain of about 9 percent. Investors who knew about the Hutchison Whampoa earnings surprise on August 5, 2010, and acted on this piece of information by buying the ADR, would make a gain of about 9 percent in one day.

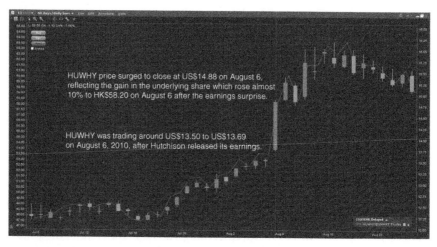

FIGURE 1.1   Hutchison Whampoa Price Chart
Source: Interactive Brokers LLC.

Figure 1.1 illustrates the price reaction of HUWHY and its underlying share Hutchison Whampoa (Stock code: 13) in the Hong Kong Stock Exchange on the days leading up to and after the earnings surprise on August 5, 2010.

A FREE LUNCH IF YOU KNOW HOW TO FIND IT

What happened to the HUWHY share price on August 6, 2010, is expected after the strong run in its underlying share price earlier that day in Asia's trading hour. What savvy traders now know is that we could have foreseen this happening if we came across such earnings news on August 5, after Asia's trading hour, to know how to interpret the results that were having a price impact.

This is almost like a free lunch in the stock market. Proponents of efficient market theory point out that the news got digested instantly and share prices adjusted immediately after a material piece of information was made known. This is true most of the time, but in this particular ADR space there is indeed some market inefficiency that we can take advantage of. This small window of opportunity occurs during the U.S. trading hour after news is released in Asia.

What we saw happening to the Hutchison Whampoa ADR price after such material earnings news was released suggests that we can indeed get a free lunch in the stock market if we know how to find it.

And it does not happen only one time, which rules out the perfect coincidence theory!

A little more than six months after the earnings surprise at Hutchison Whampoa on August 5, 2010, we got another treat from the same company!

TABLE 1.4 Hutchison Whampoa Final Results

HK$ Billion	Financial Year Ending 12/31/2010	Financial Year Ending 12/31/2009	Change
Revenue	325.9	300.5	8%
Net Profit	20.03	13.63	47%
EPS (HK$)	4.70	3.20	12%

Hutchison Whampoa's next announcement to the Hong Kong Stock Exchange, after the market closed on March 29, 2011, was similarly lucrative. The historical record shows that this second earnings report was released at 4:17 p.m. on that day in Hong Kong. See Table 1.4.

This time around, Hutchison Whampoa again managed to report a set of earnings that also topped analysts' estimates. This time Hutchison Whampoa announced an 8 percent increase in revenue to HK$325billion from HK$300 billion a year ago. Profits attributable to shareholders or net profit rose a staggering 47 percent to HK$20 billion from HK$13.6 billion in 2009. Earnings per share also rose 47 percent to HK$4.70 from HK$3.20 a year ago.

The net profit of over HK$20 billion was ahead of the market forecast of between HK$15 billion to HK$17.8 billion for 2010 according to a report by *China Daily*.

So, what was the price reaction this time around?

After getting treated to a free lunch the first time, could we realistically expect another free lunch?

Figure 1.2 illustrates the possibility of traders making relatively easy gains by making use of the earnings news on March 29 to buy into HUWHY that day and sell it the next day.

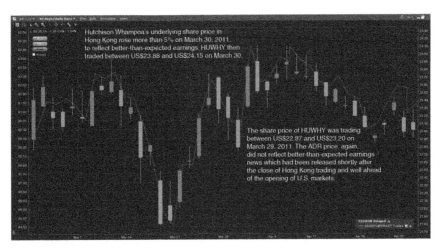

FIGURE 1.2 Hutchison Whampoa Price Chart
Source: Interactive Brokers LLC.

The share price of Hutchison Whampoa moved up significantly since the last time, when it announced that big jump in earnings that blew past the estimate. The share price of Hutchison Whampoa's underlying share in Hong Kong was trading in the range of HK$88.75 and HK$91.20, with the closing price at the lower end of the range at HK$88.80.

The ADR price also did not react to the earnings news again and Hutchison Whampoa ADR was traded between US$22.87 to US$23.20 on March 29, 2011, in the U.S. OTC market as indicated on Table 1.5.

So what happened the next day?

On March 30, 2011, Hutchison Whampoa's share price in Hong Kong reacted to the better than expected earnings news and recorded a gain of more than 5 percent. This gain is not as large as the first time but is nevertheless still considered a big gain.

This time Hutchison Whampoa ADR rose almost 5 percent to US$24.12 on the next trading day of March 30, 2011. Smart traders who had access to Hutchison Whampoa earnings news on March 29 also made a bundle buying HUWHY on March 29 and selling it the next day after the price reaction.

So, we are now two for two, making money using the after-market earnings news of Hutchison Whampoa shares listed in Hong Kong. We are making money in the U.S. markets using news from the ADR's home market before everyone else in the home market has a chance to react. This is like using tomorrow's news to trade on today's earnings. What a good feeling!

But can we expect more? After two consecutive periods producing earnings that top analysts' estimates, can we continue to profit from Hutchison Whampoa's earnings news?

The answer is a definite "Yes." That does not mean that the company must be able to deliver an earnings surprise every time. If such a trend continues, it will become expected news and the price impact will not be great. So, the next period we are in for another surprise (or rather a shock!).

TABLE 1.5 Price Range of Hutchison Whampoa Share Price and its ADR Equivalent Price Adjusted for ADR Ratio and Exchange Rate in HK$ on the Days before and after the Earnings Surprise

Date	Actual Underlying Share Price			Equivalent ADR Price (adjusted) ADR Price in Bracket (US$)		
	High	Low	Close	High	Low	Close
03/28/2011	92.00	89.35	90.70	91.02(23.34)	90.24(23.14)	90.24(23.14)
03/29/2011	91.20	88.75	88.80	90.41(23.20)	89.13(22.87)	89.94(23.08)
03/30/2011	93.60	91.20	93.35	93.99(24.15)	92.93(23.88)	93.87(24.12)

Yes, our ability to achieve a trading edge continues with after-market news from Asia, but this time we will have to be able to act on a worse than expected earnings results. See Table 1.6.

Hutchison Whampoa announced its first half result after the market closed on August 4, 2011. For the first six months of 2011, Hutchison Whampoa reported revenue growth of 26 percent from HK$148.8 billion in the corresponding period of 2010 to HK$187.4 billion. Profit attributable to shareholders grew a whopping 632 percent to HK$46.3 billion from only HK$6.3 billion the year before. Although net profit grew very strongly, the result was significantly below the average HK$51.39 billion forecast of five analysts surveyed by Dow Jones Newswires at that time. A closer examination of the financial statements, as shown in Table 1.7, reveal that the bulk

TABLE 1.6 Hutchison Whampoa Interim Results

HK$ Billion	Half-Year Ending 6/30/11	Half-Year Ending 6/30/10 (restated)*	Change
Revenue	187.4	148.8	26%
Net Profit	46.30	6.33	632%
EPS (HK$)	10.86	1.48	632%

*2010 results have been restated to reflect the Group's early adoption of HKAS 12 and the adoption of Husky Energy's new accounting policy in 2010, both with retrospective effects.

TABLE 1.7 Breakdown of Hutchison Whampoa Profit

HK$ Billion	Half-Year Ending 6/30/11	Half-Year Ending 6/30/10 (restated)	Change
Profit attributable to shareholders, before property revaluation and profits on disposal of investments and others	8.71	5.47	59%
Property revaluation after tax	0.40	0.86	–53%
Profit attributable to shareholders, before profits on disposal of investments and others	**9.12**	**6.33**	**44%**
Profits on disposal of investments and others after tax	37.2		
Profit attributable to shareholders	**46.30**	**6.33**	**632%**

of the profit came from investment property revaluations and the disposal of investments. Hutchison Whampoa's share price closed at HK$90.35 in Hong Kong on August 4 before its financial results were released.

August 4, 2011, was also remembered as the day when the Dow Jones Industrial Average Index plunged more than 500 points or about 5 percent.

Hutchison Whampoa's ADR listed on the Pink Sheets naturally dived 5 percent to close at US$22.27 from US$23.45 a day before. While the price dropped heavily, its drop was actually in line with the broader market sell-off. It did not reflect the impact of the company specific news that would drive share price down even further. As a steeper-than-market fall would be expected when the market resumes in Hong Kong the next day after such an earnings shock, we could short sell the Hutchison Whampoa ADR on August 4 to take advantage of the new information not yet reflected in its share price. See Table 1.8.

As expected, Hutchison Whampoa's share price plunged more in percentage terms than the broader market drop on the next day, August 5. The share price ended down HK$82.90 on August 5, a drop of 8.2 percent. As a result, Hutchison Whampoa's ADR opened at US$21.20 and traded as low as US$20.75 on August 5 in the United States.

Traders who were alerted to Hutchison Whampoa's disappointing earnings results acted by shorting the Hutchison Whampoa ADR on August 4. A sale of HUWHY at US$22.27 on August 4, followed by a short covering at US$21.20 the next day, would have resulted in a gain of 4.8 percent.

This sounds as easy as the previous two earnings news. However, we must be able to interpret the results accurately on this third time around because the market also suffered a big drop of about 5 percent on August 4. This is a tougher scenario to handle as one needs to know how the Hong Kong stock market in general, as represented by the Hang Seng Index, would react the next day after the Dow Jones Industrial Average dropped

TABLE 1.8 Price Range of Hutchison Whampoa Share Price and its ADR Equivalent Price Adjusted for ADR Ratio and Exchange Rate in HK$ on the Days before and after the Earnings Shock

Actual Underlying Share Price				Equivalent ADR Price (adjusted) ADR Price in Bracket (US$)		
Date	High	Low	Close	High	Low	Close
08/03/2011	91.30	90.00	91.15	91.82(23.56)	89.95(23.08)	91.39(23.45)
08/04/2011	92.20	89.40	90.35	91.20(23.40)	86.80(22.27)	86.80(22.27)
08/05/2011	84.30	81.70	82.90	83.21(21.35)	80.87(20.75)	82.62(21.20)

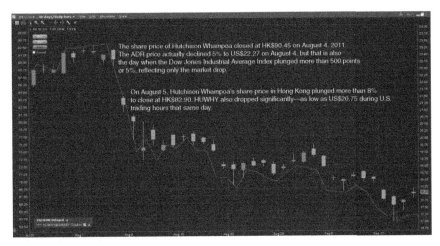

FIGURE 1.3   Hutchison Whampoa Price Chart
Source: Interactive Brokers LLC.

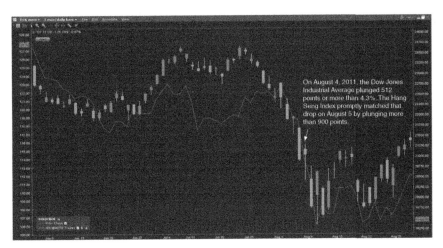

FIGURE 1.4   Dow Jones Industrial Average and Hang Seng Index Price Chart
Source: Interactive Brokers LLC.

more than 500 points. If the Hong Kong market did not experience an equal or more percentage drop than the U.S. market, such a trick may not work.

Figure 1.3 shows the price of HUWHY dropping 5 percent on August 4, followed by another 4.8 percent drop on August 5 after the earnings shock caused the Hong Kong underlying share price to drop over 8 percent.

Figure 1.4 illustrates the correlation between the Dow Jones Industrial Average (represented by DJX Index) versus the Hang Seng Index of Hong Kong.

TRADING AT TODAY'S PRICE USING TOMORROW'S NEWS

In the part of the world where I grew up, the Chinese newspapers published an evening edition of tomorrow's daily. These evening editions typically went to print around 5:00 p.m. and the papers were generally available on sale a little after 6:00 p.m. The slogan used by one of the best-selling evening papers was "Knowing Tomorrow's News Today." The sales pitch is that readers were able to know what tomorrow's headlines will be that night!

In the stock market, we always dream of being able to know tomorrow's news today so that we can buy or sell ahead of tomorrow's news and make a risk-free profit.

Using material price moving after-market news from Asia and then buying or selling Asian ADRs that are listed in the United States before the start of trading the next day (i.e., during the night time in Asia or the day time in the United States depending on where you are) will almost render us risk-free profits if we know how to interpret such news.

The examples presented in this chapter are not limited to one company. There are so many ADRs listed in the United States that we can employ the same tactic to get our free lunch in the stock market.

Therefore, we can indeed trade on tomorrow's news using today's price.

SUMMARY

This chapter used Hutchison Whampoa ADR as an example of how we can use after-market news from Asia to gain an edge trading ADRs profitably during U.S. market hours. We achieve the trading edge by accurately interpreting overlooked earnings news released after the Asian market closes before most people have a chance to act on it.

But what are ADRs? Why can we use them to trade profitably? In the next chapter, we discuss what ADRs are, look at different types of ADRs, and which ADRs are those we should keep an eye on to make money after news from Asia has been announced.

CHAPTER 2

What Are ADRs?

A t a time of uneven economic growth in different parts of the world, it would not be wise for investors to invest their money in a single market. As the old rule of thumb goes: One should never put all their eggs in one basket.

The breakneck pace of growth in the emerging economies, such as the BRICs—Brazil, Russia, India, and China—is envied by the rest of the world, so who doesn't want to invest into those markets and ride the economic booms there?

INVESTING OFFSHORE

There are many channels for investors to invest offshore. On one hand, you could open an offshore trading account with your brokerage firm, and invest directly wherever you want.

On the other hand, there are also securities called depository receipts (DRs). DRs are an investment tool that enables investors to gain exposure to companies that are listed on the other side of the globe.

A depository receipt is a type of negotiable instrument that is traded in a stock exchange. It represents ownership interest, typically in the form of ordinary shares, in another security of a foreign company listed on foreign stock markets. Depository receipts traded in American stock markets are known as American Depository Receipts, or ADRs.

ADRs have been in existence over 80 years in the United States. They were first created by J.P. Morgan in 1927 to facilitate American investments in British-based companies that were floated on the London Stock

Exchange. ADRs allow investors to buy foreign shares without having to go through the hassle of cross-border transactions in different trading time zones. In addition, investors do not have to worry about liquidity and dividend conversion, while at the same time maintaining some other benefits of investing internationally.

In a nutshell, investing in ADRs is similar to buying stock directly in a foreign-listed company. Generally, the price of an ADR will move in tandem with the underlying shares that are traded in foreign exchanges except for a single-listed ADR. A single-listed depository receipt is a DR whose underlying share is not publicly traded in the issuer's home market. The DR is listed and traded only in the DR market.

Holding ADRs will entitle investors to dividends declared by the companies. However, investors will incur currency risks, among other things. For instance, investors will see their dividend check from a Hong Kong-based firm shrink a fair bit when the U.S. dollar appreciates against the Hong Kong dollar.

An example of an ADR is CHL, which is an ADR issued against China Mobile Ltd. CHL is listed on the New York Stock Exchange (NYSE). China Mobile is the largest telecommunication company in China and the telco is listed on the Hong Kong Stock Exchange. However, China Mobile's ADRs, under the DR symbol CHL, are also traded in the United States.

CHL has a ratio of one for five. This means that one ADR unit of China Mobile represents five ordinary shares of the telecommunication firm. Table 2.1 provides the basic information about the China Mobile ADR.

By investing in China Mobile's ADR, investors gain direct exposure to the biggest telecommunication firm in China with a subscriber base of over 900 million and growing (with growth at double-digit rates).

An ADR is typically created when American banks purchase a block of shares from the company or from the primary market, bundle the shares

TABLE 2.1 China Mobile ADR

DR Symbol	CHL
CUSIP	16941M109
DR Exchange	New York Stock Exchange
DR ISIN	US16941M1099
Ratio	1:5
Depository	BNY Mellon
Effective Date	Oct 16, 1997
Underlying ISIN	HK0941009539
Underlying SEDOL	6073556
Country	China
Industry	Mobile Telecom

Source: BNY Mellon (www.adrbnymellon.com).

into groups and reissue them on the New York Stock Exchange (NYSE), the American Stock Exchange (AMEX), or the NASDAQ. The depository bank sets the ratio of U.S. ADRs per primary market share. This ratio can be anything less than or greater than 1. The ratio is adjusted so that it is high enough to show substantial value and at the same time low enough to attract the participation of retail investors.

If, for example, ABC Company trades at HKD 5, an ADR with a ratio of 1 to 1 would trade at less than US$1.00 and be classified as a penny stock. As many investors avoid penny stocks, the ADR ratio would have to be much higher than one to attract enough investor participation. Because of this, an ADR typically represents quite a few ordinary shares. The most common price range of an ADR is between $10 and $100.

TYPES OF ADRS

ADRs come in different types depending on whether they are sponsored and where they can be traded. One or more depository banks, according to market demand, can issue unsponsored depository receipts without a formal agreement with the underlying company.

A Level 1 ADR

Level 1 is the most basic type of ADR. It is not listed on any U.S. exchanges and can be traded only in the over-the-counter (OTC) market. Level 1 ADRs are not subject to very stringent regulations from the Securities and Exchange Commission (SEC). They represent shares of foreign companies that do not qualify for a U.S. exchange listing or choose not to list on the exchange.

Foreign companies with Level 1 ADRs need not register with the SEC if most of their shares trade on a foreign market and they post certain disclosure information in English on their websites or foreign regulatory databases that are readily accessible to U.S. investors. International companies use Level 1 ADRs to provide U.S. investors with convenient access to their securities.

There are two types of Level 1 ADR: sponsored and unsponsored. A sponsored ADR program is undertaken by the issuer of the deposited securities, namely the company. The company will enter into a deposit agreement with a depository that agrees to issue ADRs against the deposit of the company's shares that are floated on its home market.

Under a sponsored program, the issuer can exercise control over the terms and operation of the ADR program. Sponsored ADRs are issued by a single depository and cannot be duplicated by another depository.

On the other hand, an unsponsored ADR is set up by depository banks without participation from the issuer. There is no limit on the number of unsponsored ADR programs that can be established and consent from the issuer is not required.

A Level 2 ADR (Listed ADR)

A Level 2 ADR is always sponsored and is listed on an exchange or quoted on the NASDAQ. These ADRs are subjected to stricter SEC regulations that all listed companies need to comply with. They must also make sure that they meet the exchange's listing requirements or they may face delisting or be forced to downgrade the ADR program.

Level 2 ADR issuers are required to file a Form 20-F registration statement. Form 20-F is a form issued by the SEC that must be completed by all foreign private issuers. It calls for the submission of an annual report within six months of the end of the company's fiscal year. The information requirement of Form 20-F is not as strict as for U.S. domestic companies. Nevertheless, the issuer has to reconcile its financial statements according to IFRS (International Financial Reporting Standard) or U.S. GAAP (Generally Accepted Accounting Principles).

A Level 3 ADR (Public Issues)

A Level 3 ADR is also always sponsored. This is the most prestigious type of ADR. The foreign company is actually issuing shares to raise capital when issuing a Level 3 ADR. Publicly issued ADRs require the most stringent adherence to SEC rules.

SETTING UP A RESTRICTED PROGRAM

One unique feature of ADRs is that the issuers of such securities may set up a restricted program to have the trading of the ADRs limited to only certain individuals.

There are two SEC rules that allow this type of issuance of shares in the United States: Rule 144A and Regulation S. ADR programs operating under one of these two rules make up about one-third of all issued ADRs.

Nonetheless, this type of ADR tends to have low liquidity as only selected individual investors hold the securities. See Table 2.2.

TABLE 2.2 Summary of ADR Types

	Level 1	Level 2	Level 3	Rule 144A	Reg. S
Description	OTC	Listed	Public Issue/Listed	U.S. Private Placement	Non-U.S. Private Placement
Objective	Broaden U.S. investor base with existing shares.	Broaden U.S. investor base with existing shares.	Raise funds in U.S. and broaden U.S. investor base.	Raise funds in U.S. from qualified institutional buyer.	Raise funds outside of U.S.
Accounting/ Disclosure	Home Exchange	U.S. GAAP	U.S. GAAP	Home Exchange	Home Exchange
U.S. Reporting Requirement	Exempt	Form 20-F	Form 20-F	None	None
Liquidity	Low	Medium/ High	High	Limited	Limited

Source: ADR Reference Guide—J.P. Morgan, February 2005.

PRIMARY EXCHANGE VERSUS OTC MARKETS

Most ADRs are traded in the OTC markets, as the requirements for listing there are the lowest. There are also many companies who do not actually have any sponsored ADR program but find their ADR listed and traded in the United States.

Any depository bank can unilaterally establish an unsponsored ADR program in anticipation of, or in response to, investor and broker demand in the United States for such issuer's equity securities. Depository banks are willing to establish unsponsored ADR programs because they will generate fee-based revenues from the issuance and cancellation of the ADR.

Those ADRs listed on primary exchanges, such as the New York Stock Exchange or NASDAQ, are usually sponsored by the underlying companies and are subject to stringent reporting requirements. As company announcements have to be made in a timely manner, news about such companies, especially the larger ones, is usually captured by the media not too long after the announcements are made to the U.S. authorities.

Unsponsored ADRs that are primarily listed on the OTC market do not release company announcements to the U.S. authorities, because some underlying companies may not even be aware their ADRs have been quoted. Due to these reasons, many announcements or news made in the underlying company's home exchange are not made available in the United States in a timely manner.

Due to the characteristics of ADRs listed in the primary exchanges and OTC markets, it is not difficult to figure out that opportunities to make money from post-market-hours news from Asia are more readily available in unsponsored OTC-listed ADRs than exchange-listed ADRs. However, the not-so-well-known ADRs listed in the exchanges also provide traders opportunities to make money using this strategy. Bigger ADRs listed in the exchange will also most likely have stock options quoted as well. This provides traders an added benefit of being able to leverage their positions on such a trade.

HOW ARE ADRS PRICED VERSUS UNDERLYING SHARES?

When an investor buys ADRs, their broker can either purchase existing ADRs or create new ones. New ADRs are created when the broker purchases the underlying ordinary shares in the home market and then requests the shares be delivered to the depository bank's custodian in that country. The custodian will notify the depository bank on the same day. After notification, the new ADRs are issued and delivered to the initiating broker, who then delivers the depository receipts evidencing the shares to the investor.

Issuance and Cancellation of ADRs

Once these new units of ADRs are issued, they are tradable in the United States and can be freely sold to other investors just like any other U.S. security. These ADRs may be sold to subsequent U.S. investors by simply transferring them from the existing depository receipt holder (seller) to another depository receipt holder (buyer). This transaction is generally known as an intra-market transaction. An intra-market transaction is settled in the same manner as any other U.S. security transaction—on the third business day after the trade date and typically through The Depository Trust Company (DTC). The settlement of such a trade is in U.S. dollars. According to Bank of New York Mellon Corporation, a leading issuer of ADRs, intra-market trading accounts for approximately 95 percent of all depository receipt trading in the market today.

When an investor sells ADRs, their broker can either do so in the U.S. stock markets, or get the depository bank to exchange the ADRs for the underlying ordinary shares held in custody, and then proceed to sell these shares in the home market. When these ADRs are exchanged for underlying shares, the depository bank effectively cancels the ADRs. To settle the trade, the U.S. broker will surrender the depository receipt to the depository bank with instructions to deliver the shares to the buyer in the home market. The depository bank will cancel the depository receipt and instruct the custodian to release the underlying shares and deliver them to the local broker who purchased the shares. The broker will arrange for the foreign currency to be converted into U.S. dollars for payment to the depository receipt holder.

There are traders who look for spreads between the home market's underlying securities price and the associated ADRs' traded price, so they can arbitrage. Arbitrage involves the simultaneous purchase or sale of ADRs and the sale or purchase of the underlying securities in the home market, creating or cancelling the ADRs in order to achieve a riskless profit. This is possible when there is a large price discrepancy, after adjusting for the foreign exchange rate and ADR ratio, between the ADR and the underlying security in the primary market. The existence of ADR conversion services by a number of U.S. brokers facilitates the easy redemption and creation of ADRs, and thus facilitates arbitrage activities whenever they exist for a short period.

Nevertheless, the continuous buying and selling of depository receipts in either market tends to keep the price differential between the local and U.S. markets to a minimum.

As a result, about 95 percent of depository receipt trading is done in the form of intra-market trading and does not involve the issuance or cancellation of a depository receipt.

TRADING ADRS IN ASIA

In September 2010, the Singapore Stock Exchange (SGX) launched ADR trading through its GlobalQuote platform. GlobalQuote is an initiative by the Singapore Stock Exchange that provides quotation and trading for international securities such as ADRs, depository receipts, and depository shares of companies that are already listed on other exchanges. According to the exchange, this platform offers investors transparent price discovery and efficient share depository services in a well-regulated marketplace. The process for trading securities listed on GlobalQuote is similar to that of trading securities on SGX.

The ADRs traded on SGX are fungible. This means that investors can buy them in Singapore and sell them in the United States, or vice versa.

In addition, the dual-listed ADRs are also fully fungible with their common shares listed in the overseas market. This means we can also create and cancel ADRs just like those listed on the U.S. markets.

While the introduction of ADR trading in Asia through the Singapore Stock Exchange GlobalQuote platform allows traders to act on news released in Asia during Asian market hours, it does not enhance or impact our capability to utilize after-market news to trade on U.S.-listed ADRs.

Trading ADRs in Singapore is actually more useful for investors planning to trade on news of single-listed ADRs released during Asian trading hours where the underlying shares are not listed in Asia.

ADRS WITH A GREATER CHINA REGION THEME

According to information provided by BNY Mellon, there are close to 600 ADRs with issuers from the Greater China region that includes mainland China, Hong Kong, and Taiwan. If we include other companies with a Greater China region theme, such as those from the southeast Asian countries of Singapore, Malaysia and so on, the number is even higher.

As mentioned earlier in this chapter, opportunities to make money from ADRs using after-market-hour news are most likely to be found in smaller exchange-listed ADRs and ADRs listed in the OTC markets. In the following pages, we take a look at ten companies with a Greater China theme—all have ADRs traded in the United States. Some of these companies may be better known and some of them not so well-known to most investors outside of the Asia region. But they may just be the companies that active traders who wish to profit from such an information edge should keep on their stock-watch list:

1. China Petroleum & Chemical Corporation (Sinopec)
2. Sinopec Shanghai PetroChemical Company Ltd.
3. Yanzhou Coal Mining Company Ltd.
4. Esprit Holdings Ltd.
5. Huaneng Power International Inc.
6. Lenovo Group Limited
7. China Shenhua Energy Company Limited
8. Genting Berhad
9. Hyflux Ltd.
10. AU Optronics

China Petroleum & Chemical Corporation (Sinopec)

China Petroleum & Chemical Corporation—better known as Sinopec (386 HK)—is a state-owned, full-fledged oil and gas conglomerate with operations in both upstream activities, including exploration and production, and downstream business (for instance, crude oil refining and petrochemicals).

Sinopec was ranked the fifth largest company in terms of sales in Forbes Global 2000 in 2011. The government holds a 55.06 percent equity stake in the company through Sinopec Group, which is based in Beijing, the capital of China.

Sinopec is among the top three oil and gas companies in China. The other two are PetroChina Company Ltd. and CNOOC Ltd., both of which are also state-owned and publicly listed companies.

Comparing these three oil majors, Sinopec has more capacity in terms of downstream activities. It is China's largest producer and marketer of oil products (wholesale and retail of gasoline, diesel, jet fuel), and the number one supplier of major petrochemical products, including intermediates, synthetic resin, synthetic fiber, synthetic rubber, and fertilizer. On the upstream, Sinopec is considered the second largest crude oil producer after PetroChina.

In October 2000, the Chinese-based oil leader made its initial public offer (IPO) in Hong Kong, New York, and London with a total issuance of 16.78 billion H shares, including ADRs in the United States.

Nine months later, Sinopec sought listing on the Shanghai Stock Exchange. On August 8, 2001, Sinopec successfully floated 2.8 billion A shares in Shanghai, making it one of the first few A plus H share dual-listed, state-owned enterprises in China; among other such companies are PetroChina, and the state-owned banks, such as Bank of China, Industrial Commercial Bank of China, and Construction Bank of China.

Currently, there are 96 such Chinese companies that have dual-listed status whose A shares are floated in China and meant only for the Chinese nationals, while their H shares are listed on the Hong Kong Stock Exchange for foreign investors, including people in the special administrative region.

Sinopec's earnings have been on a steady climb between the financial year ended Dec 31, 2006, (FY2006) and FY2010. Sinopec's net profit has grown to RMB71.8 billion FY2010 from RMB53.77 billion in FY2006. Its revenue almost doubled during the period to RMB1,913 billion from RMB1,061 billion. Earnings per share (diluted) expanded to RMB0.82 in FY2010 from RMB0.62.

Marketing and distribution of the petroleum product division is the largest income earner, generating RMB1,036 billion or 54 percent of the

TABLE 2.3 Corporate Information—China Petroleum & Chemical Corporation (Sinopec)

DR Symbol	SNP
CUSIP	16941R108
DR Exchange	New York Stock Exchange
DR ISIN	US16941R1086
Ratio	1:100
Depository	Citibank
Underlying Symbol	00386.HK

Source: BNY Mellon (www.adrbnymellon.com) and HKEx.

group's total revenue for FY2010, followed by its refining division, which contributed RMB965.5 billion or 50 percent of total revenue. See Table 2.3.

Sinopec Shanghai PetroChemical Company Ltd.

Sinopec Shanghai Petrochemical Company Ltd. (SPC), as its name suggests, is a major downstream player in China's petrochemical industry.

Veteran investors in Chinese stocks abroad should be familiar with SPC. The petrochemical group is the first Chinese-based company to make a global equity offering back in 1993. The company's shares are currently listed in Shanghai, Hong Kong, and New York.

The initial public offering then involved a total of number of 7.2 billion shares, including 4 billion non-floating A shares held by Sinopec Corp., accounting for 55.56 percent of the total shares; 720 million domestic A shares, accounting for 10 percent of the total shares and 2.33 billion oversea H shares, accounting for 32.36 percent of the total shares.

Based in Shanghai, SPC is a 55.56 percent owned subsidiary of China Petroleum & Chemical Corp (Sinopec Corp)—one of the top three state-owned petroleum conglomerates in China. SPC is one of the core subsidiaries of Sinopec Corp, which is listed in similar exchanges as the SPC.

SPC produces over 60 different types of products including a broad range of synthetic fibers, resins and plastics, intermediate petrochemical products, and petroleum products. It is one of the largest producers of ethylene—an important input for synthetic fibers, resins, and plastics.

By the end of 2010, SPC's primary crude oil refining capacity stood at 14 million tons annually—among the few major oil refiners in China. The group also has an ethylene production capacity of 845,000 tons per year, an organic chemicals production capacity of 4.29 million tons per year, a synthetic resins annual production capacity of 970,000 tons, a synthetic fiber feedstock production capacity of 1.14 million tons yearly and a synthetic

TABLE 2.4 Corporate Information—Sinopec Shanghai PetroChemical Company Ltd.

DR Symbol	SHI
CUSIP	82935M109
DR Exchange	New York Stock Exchange
DR ISIN	US82935M1099
Ratio	1:100
Depository	BNY Mellon
Underlying Symbol	00338.HK

Source: BNY Mellon (www.adrbnymellon.com) and HKEx.

fiber polymers production capacity of 590,000 tons a year. SPC also generates 2,961 MW of electricity.

Petroleum products account for about 40 percent of SPC's sales, including diesel jet oil that generates about 22.43 percent of their total sales. Meanwhile, the intermediate petrochemical products segment is the second biggest revenue generator contributing some 23.88 percent, followed by resins and plastics at about 21 percent.

In terms of earnings, SPC revenue has been on a steady climb in the past decade or so, thanks to the economic boom in China that triggered rising demand for petrochemical products that are widely used across many manufacturing industries. The petrochemical group's revenue has expanded to RMB2.77 billion for the financial year ended December 31, 2010, from barely RMB20.7 million in FY2000. However, it dipped in the red in FY2008 due to escalating crude oil prices amidst the commodity boom before the global financial crisis.

SPC incurred a net loss of RMB6.23 billion for FY2008 compared with a net profit of RMB1.63 billion, despite higher revenue of RMB59.3 billion against RMB54.25 billion the year before. The group suffered from margins being squeezed due to higher raw-material costs, mainly crude oil whose price peaked above US$140 per barrel before the onset of the U.S. credit crunch. Nonetheless, since then SPC has managed to regain its earnings growth momentums. See Table 2.4.

Yanzhou Coal Mining Company Ltd.

Yanzhou Coal Mining Company Ltd. is probably no stranger to Australian investors, where the Chinese coal miner has successfully acquired several coal-mining companies.

Given its strong balance sheet, Yanzhou Coal has been on an acquisition trail to expand and diversify its coal reserves geographically, namely in China, Inner Mongolia, and Australia. Yanzhou Coal shares are listed on the Hong Kong Stock Exchange and Shanghai Stock Exchange. The miner has also issued ADRs in New York.

Yankuang Group Co. Ltd. is the company's controlling shareholder, holding a 52.86 percent equity stake. A special commission setup by China to manage state-owned enterprises, the state-owned Assets Supervision and Administration Commission (SASAC) is the ultimate parent of Yankuang.

Yanzhou Coal's core businesses are coal mining, railway transportation, coal chemicals, electricity, and heat generation. Coal mining is the main income earner, generating 95 percent of the group's revenue.

More than 80 percent of its coal is sold at the spot market, which has allowed Yanzhou to ride the rally on coal prices in recent years. However, this could be a double-edge sword when coal prices head south.

Yanzhou Coal's earnings growth has been on the fast track since 2007, leveraging rising coal prices. Its revenue has ballooned to RMB33.9 billion for the financial year ended December 31, 2010, (FY2010) from RMB12.9 billion for FY2006. Net profit soars to RMB9.28 billion for FY2010 from RMB2.3 billion.

Amidst this impressive earnings growth, Yanzhou's share price climbed in Hong Kong to a high of HK$30 in August 2010, from slightly below HK$5 in early 2009. The share price since then has retreated and it was hovering at HK$20 in early 2011.

Yanzhou Coal's crown jewels are its coal reserves and the mining rights in China and Australia. In Australia, Yanzhou took over Felix Resources for AUD3.3 billion in late 2009. Two years later, Yanzhou Coal bought out privately owned Syntech Resources, which owns 700 million tons of the Carnaby Downs thermal coal project in Queensland in Eastern Australia. Right after closing the acquisition deal, Yanzhou Coal acquired Premier Coal in Western Australia for AUD296.8 million. Premier Coal produces 3.5 million tons of thermal coal annually and supplies a local state-owned power plant.

Yanzhou Coal did not stop there. In December 2011, Yanzhou decided to consolidate its coal mining assets in Australia. The company signed an agreement to merge a large portion of its Australian assets with Gloucester Coal (GCL), a publicly listed entity in Australia, creating the largest coal mining group in Australia. Upon completion of the merger, Yanzhou will own a 77 percent equity stake in the merged entity and GCL's shareholders will own the remaining 23 percent.

In Inner Mongolia, Yanzhou Coal bought a 51 percent equity stake of Haosheng Coal Mining for RMB6.649 billion in September 2010. The acquisition gives it instant access to 1.64 billion tons of coal resources in the Shilawusu field. Yanzhou Coal's equity share of coal resources is 838.4 million tons.

TABLE 2.5 Corporate Information—Yanzhou Coal Mining Company Ltd.

DR Symbol	YZC
CUSIP	984846105
DR Exchange	New York Stock Exchange
DR ISIN	US9848461052
Ratio	1:10
Depository	BNY Mellon
Underlying Symbol	01171.HK

Source: BNY Mellon (www.adrbnymellon.com) and HKEx.

Apart from coal, Yanzhou Coal had paid US$260 million for the acquisition of 11 potash exploration permits from Devonian Potash Inc. and eight permits from North Atlantic Potash Inc. in Canada. The permits cover a total area of about 1.3 million acres in Saskatchewan province, Canada. See Table 2.5.

Esprit Holdings Ltd.

Esprit Holdings Ltd., a clothes manufacturer that was founded in San Francisco in 1968, is listed in Hong Kong. It is one of the 49 component stocks of the Hong Kong Hang Seng Index, the benchmark of the Hong Kong Stock Exchange.

The group owns the well-known international casual apparel brand, *Esprit*, and sub-brand *edc*. Apart from apparel, Esprit Holdings' product portfolio also includes accessories such as eyewear, clothes, and shoes. In Asia, it also sells cosmetics under the brand *Red Earth* and operates Salon Esprit.

Esprit Holdings has not fared well since 2008, due partly to the slowdown in the western European economy. Seventy-nine percent of the group's revenue comes from Europe, with 17 percent from Asia Pacific, and 4 percent from North America.

The group's profit has been declining since the financial year ended June 30, 2009, (FY2009) after its earnings peaked at HK$6.45 billion for FY2008. Esprit Holdings saw its profit tumble to HK$79 million for FY2011; it was dragged down by large provisions associated with store closures and the divestment of operations in North America.

The growing competition from new brands, such as Zara and H&M, is also said to be taking sales away from Esprit Holdings, particularly in Europe.

Esprit Holdings's divestment plan in North America involves shutting down 93 retail stores. On top of that, the group also identified 80 loss-making stores to be closed in Europe and Asia. It has also decided to exit retail operations in Spain, Denmark, and Sweden.

TABLE 2.6 Corporate Information—Esprit Holdings Ltd.

DR Symbol	ESPGY
CUSIP	29666V204
DR Exchange	OTC
DR ISIN	US29666V2043
Ratio	1:2
Depository	BNY Mellon
Underlying Symbol	00330.HK

Source: BNY Mellon (www.adrbnymellon.com) and HKEx.

In terms of breakdown in the contribution by individual countries, Germany is its biggest market and generates nearly 43 percent of the group's turnover for FY2011 ended June 30, followed by Benelux at 13.7 percent, and China at 7.9 percent.

Despite falling earnings, Esprit Holdings's balance sheet remains strong. As of June 2011, the group had a net cash balance of about HK$2.71 billion. With that cash in hand, Esprit Holdings has been able to pay regular dividends.

Due to its far-from-impressive earnings performance, Esprit Holdings share price did not fare well after it reached the peak of HK$119 in October 2007. Despite its presence in China, where spending power has grown substantially as a result of increase in affluence, the fashionable apparel maker failed to ride the Chinese stocks fever from 2007 to 2008.

The stock fell to a low of HK$8.23 in September 2011. It has regained some lost ground to near HK$20 in February 2012.

Esprit Holdings is planning to invest a big sum—over HK$18 billion—to reshape the group's business model. Its annual report for FY2011 says that Esprit Holdings will focus on Europe, particularly in German-speaking DACH-countries, Benelux and France, and Asia, to grow its business going forward. See Table 2.6.

Huaneng Power International Inc.

Huaneng Power International Inc. is the largest independent power producer (IPP) in China. As of March 2011, the power producer had installed (equity based) capacity of 54,167 megawatt (MW). The installed capacity is estimated to be about 5 percent of the market share of all power produced in China.

Huaneng Power owns power plants in 18 provinces in northern, eastern, and central China. Most of its power plants are coal-fired thermal plants. Consequently, the group's earnings are highly vulnerable to the fluctuation of coal prices.

The group also owns a power asset in Singapore. Huaneng Power bought Tuas Power Ltd. in Singapore from the country's sovereign fund, Temasek Holdings, for US$3 billion in 2008. Tuas Power has capacity of about 2,670MW and contributes about 24 percent of Singapore's total power supply.

State-owned China Huaneng Group holds a direct and indirect 50.91 percent stake in Huaneng Power. The power producer was the first power company in China to get listed in New York, Hong Kong, and Shanghai.

Huaneng Power's share price climbed higher from October 2011 through March 2012 on the New York Stock Exchange. The stock gained about 60 percent, from US$16 to US$26. However, on a broader horizon of five years, Huaneng Power's share price performance is rather disappointing. The IPP's share price peaked at US$45 in October 2007 and tumbled to a low of US$15 in October 2008. The stock has yet to recoup its lost ground due mainly to its lack of profitability. IPPs in China, including Huaneng Power, are indeed facing tough challenges amidst the highly regulated operating environment in the country. Despite the severe power shortage in China, where electricity rationing is necessary in the summer, power producers could still be at a loss due to rising fuel costs.

Like the prices of other consumer essential items, such as flour and petrol, the government fixes the electricity tariff. The tariff scheme is not responsive to the fluctuation of fuel prices, namely coal.

Because of the regulated electricity tariff in China, it is difficult for IPPs to pass on the additional fuel costs to end users. Consequently, power producers often have to suffer a profit margin squeeze when fuel prices get higher or cut generation to reduce losses.

In fact, Huaneng Power suffered from a net loss of RMB4.55 billion for the financial year ended December 31, 2008, compared with a net profit of RMB6.48 billion the year before, although the group's revenue grew more than one third to RMB67.8 billion from RMB49.89 billion. The loss was mainly attributed to a nearly 47 percent jump in coal prices.

In the years after, Huaneng Power managed to return to the black but its net profit was lower compared with its level in FY2007. For FY2010 ended December 31, the IPP posted net profit of RMB3.3 billion, down 35 percent from RMB5.11 billion the year before.

To hedge its future earnings, Huaneng Power has branched out to generating renewable energy. The company has set a target to increase total capacity to 90GW by 2015 from 57GW in 2011. Of the 33GW new capacity, 75 percent will come from hydro power (10GW), gas-fired power plants

TABLE 2.7 Corporate Information—Huaneng Power International Inc.

DR Symbol	HNP
CUSIP	443304100
DR Exchange	New York Stock Exchange
DR ISIN	US4433041005
Ratio	1:40
Depository	BNY Mellon
Underlying Symbol	00902.HK

Source: BNY Mellon (www.adrbnymellon.com) and HKEx.

(8GW) and wind-power plants (5GW), boosting total clean and renewable energy exposure to at least 25 percent by then. See Table 2.7.

Lenovo Group Limited

While many thought that the prospects of personal computer (PC) manufacturing had turned gloomy, anticipating that cut-throat competition would be eroding profit margins, China-based Lenovo Group made a bold step to acquire IBM's loss-making PC division in 2005 for US$1.25 billion.

Lenovo, a homegrown PC manufacturer, had to clear numerous obstacles to complete a high-profile acquisition in the U.S. using an issue of shares and cash. The takeover exercise was met with concerns on compliance within the competition law but, more importantly, U.S. authorities were worried that the deal would pose a threat to U.S. national security.

Nonetheless, the deal was worth the effort and money. It has proven to be a good move to enhance earnings and has propelled Lenovo Group to the worlds' third biggest PC maker.

Over the years, Hong Kong-listed Lenovo Group has gained market share, making it the second largest PC manufacturer globally, after Hewlett-Packard Co. The group commands about 14 percent of the world's PC-market share.

In its home market, Lenovo Group has the lion's share: 43 percent of the Chinese PC market. Its top rivals, such as Acer and Dell, hold no more than 10 percent market share each in China.

Currently, Lenovo Group is more than just a sizable PC maker. The group has ventured into smartphone and tablet manufacturing to ride the demand boom for the devices. This is seen as a move to diversify the group's earnings mix and will possibly lift Lenovo Group into a higher growth phase again. The group is also involved in smart-TV production.

Lenovo Group achieved shipments of more than three million smartphones in the third financial quarter, ending December 31, 2011. Lenovo

TABLE 2.8 Corporate Information—Lenovo Group Limited

DR Symbol	LNVGY
CUSIP	526250105
DR Exchange	OTC
DR ISIN	US5262501050
Ratio	1:20
Depository	Citibank
Underlying Symbol	00992.HK

Source: BNY Mellon (www.adrbnymellon.com) and HKEx.

Group's products include desktops and laptops that are sold under the brand ThinkPad, and touch-screen tablets called IdeaPad, as well as smartphones.

The group's revenue has grown ten times since the acquisition of IBM's PC business. Its revenue expanded to US$21.59 billion for the financial year ending June 30, 2011, from US$2.89 billion in FY2005. However, Lenovo Group's net profit has been volatile despite its top-line growth.

The group was hit hard by the economic crisis of 2008 to 2009; it slipped into a net loss of US$226.4 million for FY2009 after it achieved a record high net profit of US$484.2 million. Its earnings have since recovered after sharp losses. For FY2011, Lenovo Group more than doubled to net profit of US$273.2 million compared with US$129.3 million.

Laptops (or notebooks) are the biggest earnings contributor to Lenovo's revenue, accounting for about 53 percent. Desktops are the second largest revenue generator, contributing about one third of Lenovo's revenue.

Lenovo was founded in 1984. It was then known as New Technology Development Inc. The group made its debut on the Hong Kong Stock Exchange in 1994. It issued American Depository Receipts (ADRs) one year after its listing in Hong Kong. Each ADR represents 20 Lenovo common shares. See Table 2.8.

China Shenhua Energy Company Ltd.

China Shenhua Energy Company Ltd. is a coal-based integrated energy group. It is the leading player in China's coal industry. The group is involved in upstream mining activities, with 9.5 billion tons of marketable resources as of June 2011, power generation, as well as railway transportation.

Shenhua Energy appears to be tasked with the mission of developing the coal basin in Western China. Shenhua is fortunate to have high-quality coal mines with what appears to be a long mining life. This gives Shenhua Energy a competitive advantage of low cost and high yield.

Its coal fields are in the provinces of Shaanxi, Shanxi, and Inner Mongolia.

In July 2011, the consortium, in which Shenhua Energy holds a 40 percent equity stake, won the bid for the Tavan Tolgoi coal project which is one of the world's biggest coking coal deposits. The other members of the consortium are a Russian syndicate, which owns 36 percent interest, and Peabody Energy of America, owning a balance of 24 percent.

Overseas, Shenhua Energy has coal mining projects in Australia and South Sumatra, Indonesia. The group holds an exploration license near Gunnedah in New South Wales that contains more than 1 billion tons of coal resources.

Riding the strong coal prices, Shenhua Energy's commercial coal production rose to 224.8 million tons in 2010 from 136.6 million tons in 2006. For the same period, the company had dispatched power increased to 131.4 billion kwh from 53.9 billion kwh.

Shenhua Energy mines coal and supplies its own coal-fired power plants. The group has 15 coal-fired power plants with total installed capacity of about 29,064 MW. It supplies about 80 percent of the coal consumed by the power plants.

The secured supply of coal enables Shenhua Energy's power plants to some extent to be shielded from volatile coal prices and supply interruptions, common problems among independent power producers in China.

Shenhua Energy has a strategy to operate power plants in areas near its coal mines. This helps to ensure easy access to its fuel supply. With upstream mining activities, Shenhua Energy is in a good position to benefit from the fast-growing energy demand in China for coal and electricity.

On top of its coal mining and power generation assets, Shenhua Energy also owns and operates five railways. One is the second longest railway, linking the western inner part of China to ports in the eastern coastal area.

The vertical and horizontal integration of Shenhua Energy has given them a competitive edge among other coal-mining companies in China.

In terms of earnings, the coal-based energy group's profit has been on an upward trend amidst the growing energy demand in China to fuel the country's economic boom.

Shenhua Energy's controlling shareholder is Shenhua Group, holding a 56.43 percent equity stake. The ultimate stakeholder of the Shenhua Group is the state-owned SASAC, a special commission that manages China's state-owned enterprises.

Shenhua Energy is one of the component stocks of the benchmark Hang Seng Index on the Hong Kong Stock Exchange. The company has also issued H-shares that are listed on the Shanghai Stock Exchange, and its ADRs quoted on OTC markets. See Table 2.9.

TABLE 2.9 Corporate Information—China Shenhua Energy Company Ltd.

DR Symbol	CSUAY
CUSIP	16942A302
DR Exchange	OTC
DR ISIN	US16942A3023
Ratio	1:10
Depository	Unsponsored (Various)
Underlying Symbol	01088.HK

Source: BNY Mellon (www.adrbnymellon.com) and HKEx.

Genting Berhad

Malaysian-based Genting Berhad is a leading casino operator in Asia Pacific with footprints in many major cities around the world. The group holds the sole casino license in Malaysia. Genting also owns one of the two casinos in Singapore and the largest number of casinos in the UK. In addition, Genting runs the Aqueduct racetrack, which has a large slot machine parlor, including electronic table games, in New York.

The group's latest mega-investment is in Miami where Genting is trying hard to lobby for a license to operate a casino in a holiday resort that features six luxurious hotel-apartments. As a start, Genting, through its subsidiary Genting Malaysia Bhd., bought *The Miami Herald* headquarters for US$236 million.

Apart from casinos, Genting owns nearly 60,000 hectares of oil palm plantations. It has a property development arm and upstream operation in the oil and gas industry, as well as power generation. The group also holds an associate stake in cruise-liner operator, Genting Hong Kong Ltd., which operates Star Cruises in Asia Pacific and Norwegian Cruise Line, a 50 percent joint ownership alongside Apollo and TPG Capital.

Genting is listed on Bursa Malaysia, the stock exchange in Malaysia. Within the group, there are several listed entities, namely Genting Malaysia Berhad, Genting International Limited, Genting Plantations Berhad, and Genting Hong Kong Limited.

Both Genting Malaysia and Genting Plantations are listed on Bursa Malaysia, while Genting International is listed in Singapore, and Genting Hong Kong in Hong Kong.

Among the subsidiaries, Genting Malaysia owns the hilltop casino in Malaysia plus 46 out of 147 casinos in the UK, and the Aqueduct racetrack in New York.

The controlling shareholder of Genting is Lim Kok Thay and his family. Kok Thay's father, the late Lim Goh Tong, founded the group. Goh Tong was

TABLE 2.10   Corporate Information—Genting Berhad

DR Symbol	GEBHY
CUSIP	372452300
DR Exchange	OTC
DR ISIN	US3724523002
Ratio	1:5
Depository	BNY Mellon
Underlying Symbol	3182.KL

Source: BNY Mellon (www.adrbnymellon.com) and Yahoo Finance.

granted the first and only casino license in Malaysia in 1969. Since then he has built the family's fortunes on the hilltop casino.

After Kok Thay took over the helm in 2007, the Genting group has been actively expanding its casino operations around the world, a move to be perceived as diversifying its earnings portfolio.

Genting's earnings growth has accelerated amidst its expansions abroad. It hit record profit for two consecutive years thanks to contributions from its casino/holiday resort in Sentosa, Singapore.

For the financial year ended December 31, 2011, Genting's net profit soared to RM2.86 billion—the highest level ever—against RM2.2 billion in the preceding year. Revenue expanded to RM19.55 billion from RM15.19 billion for FY2010.

Its hospitality division, including casino operations, is the core income stream that generated 83 percent of Genting's total revenue for FY2011. Power generation is the second, accounting for 16.5 percent of the group's revenue, and its plantations 11 percent.

A major global sell-down in the equities markets worldwide occurred when Genting's share price tumbled to a multiyear low of RM3.18 in March 2009. Since then, the stock has been on a steady climb to a historical high of RM11.98 in January 2011. See Table 2.10.

Hyflux Ltd.

Singapore-listed Hyflux Ltd. made its breakthrough in 2003 when it secured a job to build and operate the first desalination plant in Singapore. The project has given it recognition of capability in water treatment operations and has, in turn, helped the group to win more jobs outside its home base.

The 20-year, design-build-own-operate deal for the desalination plant was awarded to Hyflux's then wholly owned subsidiary, SingSpring. The plant has a capacity to supply 136,380 cubic meters of desalinated potable water a day, meeting about 10 percent of Singapore's current water consumption.

Eight years later, Hyflux again won another contract to build, own, and operate Singapore's second—and largest—seawater desalination plant, with a capacity of producing 318,500 cubic meters of water a day for a concession period of 25 years.

The new desalination plant is designed to produce 318,500 cubic meters of water per day. The key technology in the desalination process is reverse osmosis, where seawater is forced against semi-permeable membranes under pressure in a continuous flow condition.

Hyflux will also be constructing a 411MW combined cycle gas turbine (CCGT) power plant to supply electricity to the desalination plant. Excess power will be sold to the power grid.

The total project cost of the desalination plant and power plant is S$890 million. It will be funded through a combination of equity and project financing. Construction was slated to start by the fourth quarter of 2011, and the project is scheduled to commence operations by 2013.

Apart from the projects in Singapore, Hyflux's landmark projects include the world's largest seawater reverse osmosis (SWRO) plant in Magtaa, Algeria.

Hyflux currently has established its presence in major cities in China, Malaysia, India, and the Middle East, as well as some European countries, such as Sweden, Switzerland, and Germany.

Hyflux manages the long duration of its assets by engaging in capital recycling efforts and was a pioneer in the use of Singapore's business trust framework for this purpose, through the divestment of SingSpring to Temasek in 2005.

Hyflux disposed of a 70 percent equity stake in SingSpring to Temasek Holdings Ltd., the investment arm of Singapore government, leaving itself with a 30 percent equity stake in the company. This is part of the group's asset-light strategy. With the 70 percent equity stake in SingSpring together with other water treatment assets, Temasek formed a water asset trust called CitySpring Infrastructure Trust and listed the trust in Singapore. Hyflux currently still holds its 30 percent equity interest.

In 2007 Hyflux set up Hyflux Water Trust to inject 13 of its Chinese water treatment plants into the trust.

In terms of earnings growth, Hyflux has scored high since the financial year ending December 31, 2007. The company saw its revenue exceed the S$500-million mark in the financial year ended December 31, 2008, (FY2008) to S$554.2 million, a big jump from S$192.7 million for FY2007. Its net profit grew to S$59.03 million during the year from S$32.9 million. But, Hyflux's net profit was down 37 percent to S$55.7 million for FY2011 due to revenues falling 15 percent, to S$481.9 million, partly due to the Arab Spring events. See Table 2.11.

TABLE 2.11 Corporate Information—Hyflux Ltd.

DR Symbol	HYFXY
CUSIP	449034107
DR Exchange	OTC
DR ISIN	US4490341074
Ratio	1:20
Depository	Unsponsored (Various)
Underlying Symbol	E1:600.SI

Source: BNY Mellon (www.adrbnymellon.com) and Yahoo Finance.

AU Optronics

AU Optronics (AUO), the world's top LCD panel supplier, is one of the success stories of Taiwan's high-technology industry, forming the backbone of the island's economy.

The homegrown display panel manufacturer started as a TFT-LCD manufacturer called Unipac. It was then the pioneer TFT-LCD producer in Taiwan. Unipac made its debut on the Taiwan Stock Exchange in July 2000 to raise fresh capital to grow its business. One year later, the company merged with Acer Display Technology, a member of Acer group, to form AUO to gain size.

Another milestone achieved in 2002 was when AUO floated its shares in the New York Stock Exchange.

AUO has specialized in display panels. To strengthen its footing in an industry where it has to compete with South Korean producers, who tend to have technological advantages, and those in China, who leverage low labor costs, AUO continuously develops new technologies to stay ahead of its competition.

Over the years, it has diversified into various segments in the panel industry to cater to different needs; for instance, AMOLED (active-matrix organic light-emitting diode) for smartphones.

AUO's major products are the display panels for personal computers, laptops, mobile phones, and televisions. Among its key customers are Samsung, LG, Acer, and Dell, as well as China-based TCL and Haier. Interestingly, Samsung and LG Display are also AUO competitors in the world's display panel industry, along with its Taiwanese peer, Chimei Innolux Corp.

Display panels for TVs are breadwinners for AUO. TV segment accounts for about 40 percent of the group's revenue. Panels for laptops and personal computer monitors contribute some 17 percent and 16 percent, respectively.

Apart from display panels, AUO ventured into solar energy as a strategic move to participate in renewable or green energy in 2008. BenQ Solar is the brand name that AUO has created to grow its solar energy operation.

TABLE 2.12 Corporate Information—AU Optronics

DR Symbol	AUO
CUSIP	002255107
DR Exchange	New York Stock Exchange
DR ISIN	US0022551073
Ratio	1:10
Depository	Citibank
Underlying Symbol	2409.TW

Source: BNY Mellon (www.adrbnymellon.com) and Yahoo! Finance.

AUO has started solar farming in South Africa. The company is also partnering with NASDAQ-listed SunPower to construct a solar-cell fabricator in Malaysia. Upon completion in 2013, the facility is expected to generate more than 1,400 megawatts annually of high-efficiency solar cells. The two-building facility, which is about the size of seven U.S. football fields, will house 28 solar-cell production lines when fully online.

AUO currently has PV module plants in Taiwan, China, and the Czech Republic. However, solar energy has yet to bring in big money to AUO.

Despite the global increase in the usage of LCD display panels, AUO's earnings have been rather volatile after the onset of the U.S. credit crunch in the second half of 2008. The steady earnings growth in AUO seems to have been interrupted by the global financial crisis, in addition to the intensive competition that is weakening its pricing power. The company's revenue and net profit are lower.

AUO sunk into losses for the financial year ending December 31, 2011. It incurred a hefty loss of NT$61.26 billion or NT$6.94 per share. This is AUO's biggest loss since it was listed in Taiwan. The company's profit peaked at NT$56.4 billion in FY2007. Likewise, AUO share prices have not fared well due to less-than-impressive earnings. Its share price hit a historic high of US$20 in 2007 as well. See Table 2.12.

TERMINATING AN ADR PROGRAM

It is possible to terminate an ADR program. When an ADR program is terminated, it will result in cancellation of all the depository receipts, and a subsequent delisting of the ADRs from all exchanges where they are traded.

Usually the termination comes by request from the issuer, although the depository bank may also do so. The reasons for termination of ADRs can be due to corporate restructuring or a merger of the issuer. They may also be due to issuers deciding to terminate ADR programs due to cost issues. For example, Asia Satellite Telecommunications Holdings in 2008

TABLE 2.13 List of Terminated ADRs from China and Hong Kong

DR Issue	Symbol	Ratio DR: Ord Share	Sponsored/ Unsponsored	Termination Date
AIA	AAIGY	1:4	Unsponsored	June 21, 2011
APT Satellite	ATS	1:8	Sponsored	November 5, 2008
ASAT	ASTTY	1:15	Sponsored	June 18, 2010
Asia Satellite Telecommunications	AISLY	1:10	Sponsored	February 28, 2008
Brilliance China Automotive	BCAHY	1:100	Sponsored	August 31, 2009
China Gas	CGHOY	1:500	Sponsored	December 3, 2007
ChinaCast Communication	CCHYY	1:30	Sponsored	January 11, 2010
CITIC International Financial	CIIEY	1:20	Unsponsored	May 27, 2009
Corgi International	CRGIY	1:1	Sponsored	April 15, 2010
Denway Motors Ltd.	DENMY	1:50	Unsponsored	September 14, 2010
EganaGoldpfeil	EGFLY	1:300	Sponsored	July 6, 2009
Esprit Holdings	ESHDY	1:2	Unsponsored	November 17, 2009
Fu Ji Food and Catering Services	FJFCY	1:20	Unsponsored	February 17, 2011
Grand Toys International	GRINY	1:5	Sponsored	May 31, 2009
Hong Kong Construction	HKGCY	1:5	Sponsored	November 6, 2007
Huscoke Resources Holdings	HKHOY	1:20	Sponsored	July 27, 2009
Hutchison 3G Italy–Reg. S	—	1:1	Sponsored	April 30, 2009
NWS	NWSZY	1:10	Unsponsored	October 8, 2009
ONFEM	ONHLY	1:10	Sponsored	June 18, 2007
Shanghai Zhenhua Port Machinery	SZPMY	1:10	Unsponsored	August 19, 2010
SUNDAY Communications	SDAY	1:100	Sponsored	February 1, 2007
Tongjitang Chinese Medicines	TCM	1:4	Sponsored	May 4, 2011
VTech	VTKHY	1:10	Sponsored	January 21, 2011
WahKwong Shipping	WKSHY	1:5	Unsponsored	October 5, 2007

TABLE 2.13 (*Continued*)

Winsor Industrial	WIINY	1:5	Unsponsored	January 25, 2007
Xinhua Finance	XHFNY	100:1	Sponsored	April 13, 2011
Yueshou Environmental Holdings	YSHUY	1:100	Sponsored	April 3, 2009
ZhongDe Waste Technology	ZWTYY	2:1	Unsponsored	August 25, 2010

Source: BNY Mellon (www.adrbnymellon.com).

voluntarily delisted its American Depository Shares from the New York Stock Exchange and ended its ADR program due to relatively low participation and related costs.

Investors who hold ADRs are usually notified in writing more than thirty days ahead of termination. Upon receiving the termination notice, investors who hold the ADRs may elect to surrender their ADRs and take delivery of the foreign shares according to the exchange ratio. However, the investors must be able to find a broker with the capability to handle buying and selling the foreign shares if they elect to take delivery of the underlying shares. A better option would be to just sell the ADRs prior to termination and delisting.

There can be also instances of unsponsored ADRs being terminated to make way for sponsored ADRs. An example would be the unsponsored ADRs of Esprit Holdings Limited (ESHDY) being terminated and replaced by sponsored ADRs (ESPGY) when Esprit appointed BNY Mellon as its depository bank in 2009. Esprit common shares are listed in Hong Kong Stock Exchange under the code 00330.

Table 2.13 lists the ADRs from China and Hong Kong that have been delisted from U.S. markets in the recent years.

SUMMARY

This chapter introduced ADRs as securities where U.S. as well as international investors can participate in foreign shares traded outside their home markets. We went through the types of ADRs available and the mechanism as to how ADRs are created and cancelled. We also introduced ten companies from Asia which traders can take advantage of using after-hours market news.

In the next chapter, we look at how and where to find news and information that give traders an edge in buying and selling ADRs.

CHAPTER 3

Finding and Interpreting News to Enter the Market

As defined in Chapter 1, ADRs are securities that are issued by foreign-based companies and traded in the U.S. market. When a foreign company's home exchange is located in a different time zone, this could result in a time lag in information dissemination to investors in other exchanges. For instance, when a China-based firm, which is listed in Hong Kong, makes a corporate announcement after the domestic trading hour, such market sensitive information may not reach investors in New York as fast. This is mainly because of the 12-hour time difference between Hong Kong and New York.

It is exactly this time lag on information dissemination that, more often than not, has opened a window of opportunity for investors to make some quick profits.

When the issuer announces price-sensitive news after the home exchange trading hours but during U.S. market trading hours, investors who are active during U.S. market hours can actually use the news to trade on the respective ADRs.

So, where could you hunt for price-sensitive news in order to profit from it? You may not have to go far for the information that could swing share prices. You can turn to Asian news and financial websites to look for these gems!

WHERE TO LOOK FOR NEWS

There are generally two types of news that can affect a company share price in the following trading days:

1. Company-specific news.

2. Other news that may affect a company's financial performance such as changes in policies, political news, natural disasters, and so on.

Company-Specific News

For company-specific news, it is rather obvious that financial earnings, material award of contracts, mergers and acquisition announcements, and special dividends, and so on, can be price moving. All these could move share prices one way or another. But where do you go to look for such news?

Depending on where the company is listed, its primary stock exchange's official company announcement webpage is the most reliable source of news.

As most of the China-related ADRs have their primary listings on the Hong Kong Stock Exchange, we will now examine in detail how to look for information on company specific news from the Hong Kong Stock Exchange.

Hong Kong Stock Exchange

Hong Kong Exchanges and Clearing Limited (HKEx) is the holding company of The Stock Exchange of Hong Kong Limited, Hong Kong Futures Exchange Limited, and Hong Kong Securities Clearing Company Limited.

Most ADRs on Chinese companies have their primary listing in Hong Kong. HKEx is an international public financial market that accommodates listings of companies from all over the world that qualify for its listing requirements. Besides Hong Kong companies, companies from mainland China, Taiwan, Macau, and even southeast Asia are listed in HKEx.

HKEx has created a dedicated website for the dissemination of all listed company information. This news website is separate from the main HKEx website (www.hkex.com.hk) and has its own domain name (www.hkexnews.hk) and identity.

According to information provided from www.hkexnews.hk, the website covers two main areas:

1. Issuer-generated information.

   All listed companies or issuers on HKEx are required to submit company announcements through the e-Submission System to this website. Such announcements include vetted issuer documents required under the Main Board or Growth Enterprise Market (GEM) Listing Rules and non-vetted issuer documents. It also includes disclosure information filed with the Disclosure of Interests (DI) System by major shareholders or directors of listed companies in accordance. This captures all the changes in the shareholding of substantial shareholders and directors, as well as the emergence of new substantial shareholders.

2. HKEx-generated regulatory issuer information.

This includes HKEx-generated regulatory information on companies listed on the Main Board and GEM, such as status reports on delisting proceedings and suspensions, prolonged suspension status reports, and listing enforcement notices/announcements.

You should be able to find out all listed companies' official announcements from the HKExnews website.

Looking for Specific Company Announcements

Listed companies are represented by stock codes. In Hong Kong, most investors remember listed companies by their stock codes, which are comprised of up to five digits. For example, the stock code for Cheung Kong (Holdings) Ltd. is 1 (00001. HK) while the stock code for Petro China Co. Ltd. is 857 (00857. HK).

There are three ways to access listed company information from the HKExnews website.

Latest Information All listed companies' announcements in this section are sorted by the time the announcements are made to the investing public. Figure 3.1 is a snapshot from a website with the latest company information.

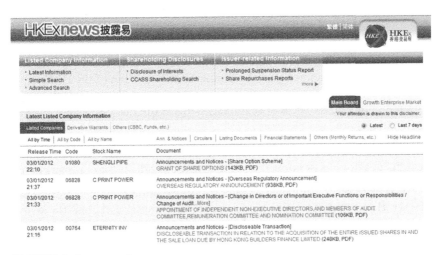

FIGURE 3.1 Latest Announcements

Source: HKEx.

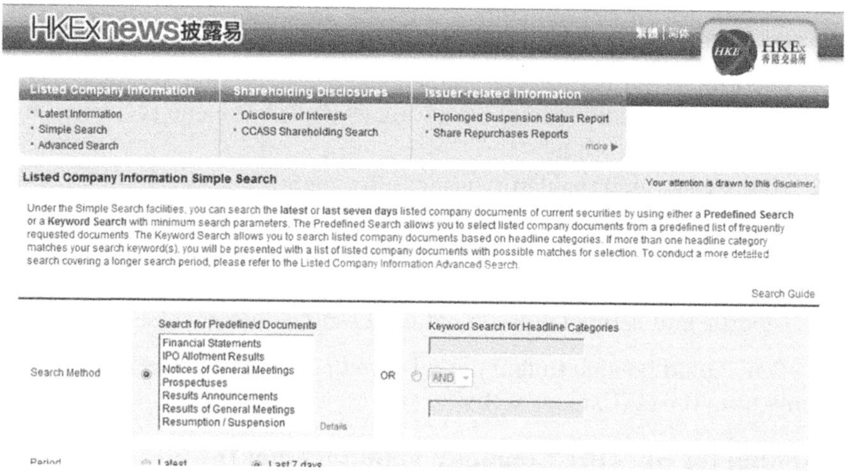

FIGURE 3.2 Simple Search

Source: HKEx.

The sorting of companies' announcements by time enables investors to immediately know what material information, which could probably swing share prices or even the general market, has been put out in the market during that day.

This is also a step to improve transparency in terms of information dissemination on HKEx.

Simple Search You can search for the latest or last seven days' listed company documents by using a predefined document search or keyword search. Figures 3.2 and 3.3 are snapshots from the Simple Search section.

For illustration, Figure 3.3 is a screenshot of a search for the latest financial statements under the Simple Search section of the HKExnews website. If you want to know all the latest financial results of listed companies announced over the last seven days, this is the place to visit.

Advanced Search An advanced search allows investors to search for all the material announcements made by a specific company. To facilitate the search, investors must know the company stock code or the company name.

For example, if you wish to look for information on China Mobile Ltd. (00941. HK), you just need to key in the stock code 941 and press the search button as illustrated in Figure 3.4.

After the search button is pressed, all documents related to China Mobile Ltd. will be displayed as in Figure 3.5.

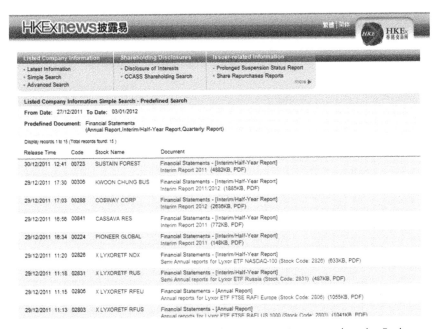

FIGURE 3.3 Search for Latest Financial Statements Announced to the Exchange Over Past Seven Days

Source: HKEx.

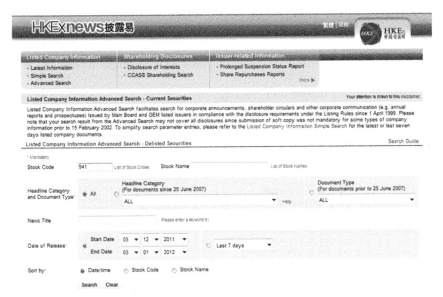

FIGURE 3.4 Advanced Search for China Mobile Announcements—Input

Source: HKEx.

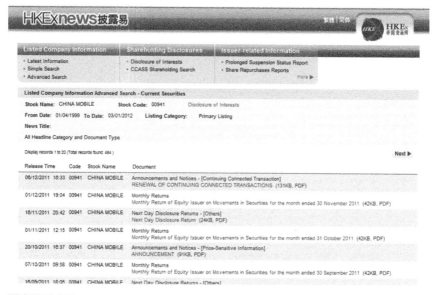

FIGURE 3.5   Advanced Search for China Mobile Announcements—Results
Source: HKExnews.

OTHER ASIAN EXCHANGES

Besides the Hong Kong Stock Exchange, there are also ADRs with their primary listings in other Asian exchanges like Taiwan, Singapore, and Malaysia.

The stock exchanges in China are rather different from others in the region. Foreign participation in the Chinese stock markets is limited and highly regulated. Basically, other than local citizens, only Qualified Foreign Institutional Investors (QFII) are permitted to invest in the Chinese stock markets. Foreign investors, including those from Hong Kong, are not allowed to trade A-shares that are listed on the Shanghai Stock Exchange and Shenzhen Stock Exchange.

The following pages offer a brief description of the official stock exchanges from a few Asian countries with significant Chinese presence.

Taiwan Stock Exchange

Taiwan Stock Exchange Corporation (TWSE) operates the Taiwan stock market. Its official website in English can be accessed at www.twse.com.tw/en/.

Company Information from Taiwan Stock Exchange

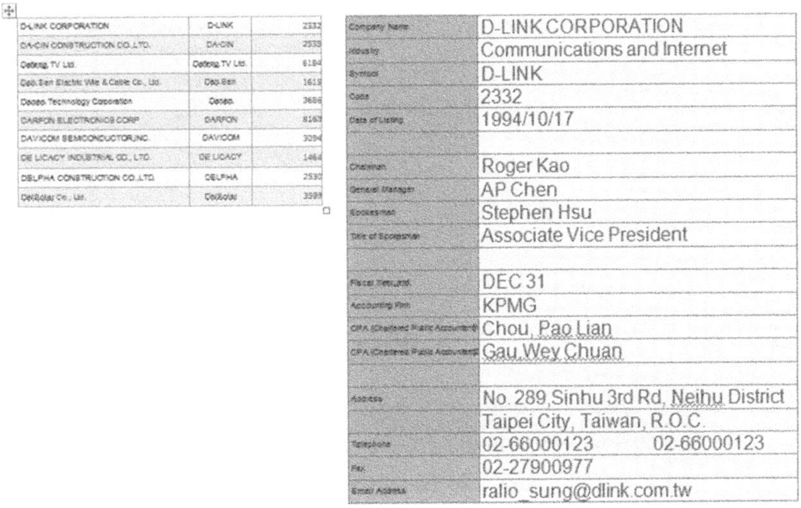

D-LINK CORPORATION	D-LINK	2332
DA-CIN CONSTRUCTION CO.,LTD.	DA-CIN	2535
Dafeng TV Ltd.	Dafeng TV Ltd.	6184
Dah San Electric Wire & Cable Co., Ltd.	Dah San	1615
Daxon Technology Corporation	Daxon	3686
DARFON ELECTRONICS CORP	DARFON	8163
DAVICOM SEMICONDUCTOR,INC.	DAVICOM	3094
DE LICACY INDUSTRIAL CO., LTD.	DE LICACY	1464
DELPHA CONSTRUCTION CO.,LTD.	DELPHA	2530
DelSolar Co., Ltd.	DelSolar	3599

Company Name	D-LINK CORPORATION	
Industry	Communications and Internet	
Symbol	D-LINK	
Code	2332	
Date of Listing	1994/10/17	
Chairman	Roger Kao	
General Manager	AP Chen	
Spokesman	Stephen Hsu	
Title of Spokesman	Associate Vice President	
Fiscal Year End	DEC 31	
Accounting Firm	KPMG	
CPA (Chartered Public Accountant)	Chou, Pao Lian	
CPA (Chartered Public Accountant)	Gau,Wey Chuan	
Address	No. 289,Sinhu 3rd Rd, Neihu District	
	Taipei City, Taiwan, R.O.C.	
Telephone	02-66000123	02-66000123
Fax	02-27900977	
Email Address	ralio_sung@dlink.com.tw	

FIGURE 3.6 Taiwan Listed Companies Information
Source: M.O.P.S.

In order to search the latest listed companies' announcements, you have to go to another website, Market Observation Post System (M.O.P.S). It can be accessed at emops.twse.com.tw/emops_all.htm. Figure 3.6 is a snapshot from M.O.P.S. displaying basic company information on companies with a starting alphabet of D (with D-Link Corporation at the top of this list). You can also search for specific company information, such as financial statements.

Singapore Exchange

Singapore Exchange Limited (SGX) operates the city-state's only integrated securities exchange and derivatives exchange, and their related clearing house. Besides Singapore companies, SGX is the home of many other Asian companies, including companies from mainland China.

It is also interesting to note that SGX provides quotation and trading of ADRs via its GlobalQuote initiative. Since ADRs traded in Singapore are the same as ADRs traded in the United States, you can hold your ADRs in either depository and still be able to buy or sell in both the Singapore and U.S. exchanges. This way, you can almost trade ADRs round-the-clock, as both stock exchanges are in different time zones with a difference of 12 hours between them.

FIGURE 3.7 SGX My Gateway

Source: SGX.

FIGURE 3.8 Malaysian Stock Exchange
Source: Bursa Malaysia.

Investors can access information on securities traded on SGX via the My Gateway page from the SGX website. My Gateway is a one-stop educational portal for retail investors. It can be accessed via www.sgx.com/mygateway. See Figure 3.7.

Malaysian Stock Exchange

Bursa Malaysia operates the stock exchange in Malaysia. Previously known as the Kuala Lumpur Stock Exchange, Bursa Malaysia was the fourth biggest exchange in terms of market capitalization in the early 1990s. In fact, there were even a few ADRs of Malaysian shares established then.

Nevertheless, the Malaysian Stock Exchange has been a pale shadow of its former self since the Asian financial crisis of the late 1990s when capital control was introduced. In recent years, Chinese companies have started to list on the Malaysian Stock Exchange.

Bursa Malaysia has a website (www.bursamalaysia.com) where investors can search for information about listed companies. Figure 3.8 displays the company announcements page of Bursa Malaysia.

OTHER NEWS SOURCES

Besides company specific news, there are other news and events which may affect share prices. Some of this news includes:

- Announcements of price changes in controlled price items such as gasoline price, electricity price, and so on.
- Announcements of changes in government policies.
- Political news that is sensitive to some politically linked companies.

When such news is not prominently broadcasted over international news media, it is quite likely that ADRs that can benefit or suffer from such news will not see a significant change in prices.

In order to gain an edge in trading ADRs from the Greater China region, it is important for traders to keep a list of websites that may first publish the news before the major Western media get a hold of it.

Here are a few news websites that you may want to keep in mind:

Shanghai Securities News (english.cnstock.com)

Shanghai Securities News is China's leading financial newspaper and the China Securities Regulatory Commission's government-designated channel for disclosure of Chinese-listed companies. Daily coverage of SSN focuses on the securities markets and company news, but also covers banking,

FIGURE 3.9 Shanghai Securities News Main Page

Source: Shanghai Securities News.

insurance, foreign exchange, futures, and real estate. Shanghai Securities News is owned by Xinhua News Agency, the official press agency of the government of the People's Republic of China.

China Securities Journal (www.cs.com.cn/english/)

The *China Securities Journal* is a national securities newspaper sponsored by Xinhua News Agency. This newspaper covers the securities and the financial markets in China.

Finet Hong Kong (www.finet.hk)

Finet Web Products are packaged financial information products for individual investors worldwide. The group has bundled its content offerings, including real-time market data on stocks, warrants, options and futures, and analysis tools for the Hong Kong and U.S. markets, into modular application tools and information packages to provide various web-based teletext and stock quotation services to individual investors.

AAStocks.com (www.aastocks.com)

AAStocks.com Limited is a premier one-stop solutions provider devoted to the development and production of advanced financial technology solutions, information services, and system integration for both corporate

FIGURE 3.10 AAStocks—Financial News
Source: AAStocks.com Limited.

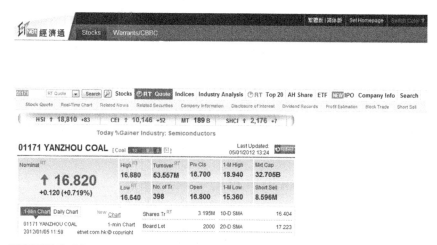

FIGURE 3.11   ET Net Limited—Stock Quotation and News
Source: ET Net Limited (www.etnet.com.hk).

clients and individual investors in the Asia Pacific regions. Figure 3.10 is a screenshot displaying the news section of AAStocks.com.

ET Net Limited (www.etnet.com.hk)

ET Net Limited is a subsidiary of Hong Kong Economic Times Group, the leading Chinese financial newspaper in Hong Kong since 1988. ET Net provides a comprehensive range of real-time equities and derivatives quotations, financial news, commentaries, securities market research information and Hong Kong–listed company information to the professional market and retail investors in Hong Kong.

Figure 3.11 shows the stock quotation page of ET Net.

Quamnet (www.quamnet.com)

Quamnet.com is a popular financial website in Hong Kong that is famous for its independent, in-depth stock analysis and market-beating investment recommendations. Investors can also access its online video on QuamTV.

FACTORS AFFECTING SHARE PRICE

Share price will move significantly when a new piece of information is totally unexpected. The price mechanism of the stock market is simple. It fluctuates with the demand and supply of a company's shares on the open market. Naturally, share price will go higher when there is a surge in buying interest or demand for a particular stock and, at the same time, the existing shareholders are not willing to part with their shares. Likewise, when investors are dumping shares on the open market and there is no demand to absorb the selling pressure, the share price will head south.

There are many factors that can affect the demand and supply equation and hence affect share price. You want to look for news that contains factors that can impact share price.

Macroeconomic Factors

Macroeconomic factors can have an impact on the stock market and individual share price. The impact will be even more significant when the macroeconomic events are unexpected (for instance, the central bank decides to raise interest rates to curb inflation but the market anticipated the policymakers to cut interest rates to boost economic growth).

Events that can lead to change in expectations include changes in:

- Monetary policies
- Inflation numbers
- Employment figures
- Consumption numbers
- Business confidence
- Foreign exchange reserves
- Trade figures

The greater the difference between the actual change in policy or the economic statistics and the market consensus view, the greater the share price movements.

Changes in Government Policies

Government policies have a great impact on share prices, especially when the changes in policies or new policies announced are totally unexpected.

In developing countries, where governments often implement price control policies on essential items such as petrol, sugar, and flour, any changes in controlled price levels or mechanisms will have a significant impact on the share price of companies in the affected industries.

Changes in regulatory environment can also have a great impact on share prices of companies affected by such changes in regulation. For example, the liberalization of the domestic banking industry allows foreign players to capture a slice of the local market by setting up operations in the country. When this happens, the share prices of the local banks are likely to head down amidst concerns over rising competition from foreign banks, which are likely to lure customers away from the domestic banks. And that would mean a possible fall in the domestic banks' earnings.

Another example of changes in public policy is abolishment of import duties for certain raw materials that are used by manufacturers. A situation like this would be positive news for the manufacturers as the lack of import duty helps them save on costs, which in turn boosts profits.

Natural Disasters

Natural disasters such as earthquakes, typhoons, tsunamis, snowstorms, and so on, can have a great impact—especially when such disasters are devastating—on share prices because such events are normally unexpected.

It is worth noting that there could be a contagion effect that spreads outside the disaster hit country. One recent example is the severe earthquake and tsunami in Japan in 2011. The disaster not only brought down the share prices on the Tokyo Stock Exchange, but also the publicly listed car manufacturers operating outside Japan. This was due to supply chain disruption.

Car manufacturers in Europe, the United States, and other parts of Asia had to halt production because the disaster had disrupted the supply of Japanese auto parts to the world. The semiconductor and electronics industries also faced similar problems in the wake of the 2011 earthquake/tsunami in Japan.

Mergers and Acquisitions

Mergers and acquisitions announcements tend to have a big and immediate impact on share price if the acquisition price deviates substantially from the market price. If an acquiring company launches a takeover of a target company at a huge premium to market price, it is reasonable to assume that the target company's share price will rise nearer to the takeover price.

Earnings Surprises or Shocks

When a listed company announces a set of earnings that deviates substantially from market expectations, the share price of the company will move up or down depending on the direction of the deviation. Investors generally use the average or median analysts' earnings estimates as a gauge of market expectations.

Corporate Exercises, such as Rights Issues, Bonus Issues, and Stock Splits

Investors do not generally view a corporate exercise, such as rights issues, favorably. Rights issues require additional investment from shareholders and not all shareholders are prepared to put in more money. Shareholders who do not take up rights issues will also see their stake diluted. Many companies set the rights issue price at a significant discount to the current market price of the share. This often causes the share price to drop.

Bonus issues, where a company rewards shareholders with additional free shares or stock splits, can sometimes lead to price increases in the share price (after adjusting for the effect of bonus or splits) even though in theory nothing has really changed.

Other Company-Specific Announcements or Events

Company-specific announcements or events may also cause the share price to go up or down. Examples of these announcements include the introduction of new products and services, announcements on sales figures on certain major products and services, and announcements of substantial contracts or changes in chief executives or top management of the company.

HOW TO INTERPRET THE NEWS

After you realize what factors lead to changes in share price, you have to be able to interpret news that can potentially have a huge impact on share price. Your ability to interpret the news correctly determines whether you can make use of the news from Asia and trade profitably in the United States through ADRs: information is power!

You must also look for news not yet picked up by major Western media outlets, since the impact of the share price is already reflected in the price of the ADRs. The biggest companies from China are often well covered by Western media due to their sheer size and global interest. Nevertheless, there can be a few hours' lead time after the news is first made available in local exchanges or before the news is transmitted by major Western media outlets. In such circumstances, the ability to comprehend a local language like Chinese gives traders a huge advantage in profiting. However, those who do not understand local languages can still find such news if they try hard enough or make use of web language translators.

So what news can we use to make money and how do we best interpret it? Not all price-moving news is useful and, if the news is well covered, the opportunities for trading disappear. Also, as pointed out previously in this chapter, there is also news that can occur on an irregular basis, news that traders cannot really plan for.

However, there are two major categories of news that traders *can* prepare for and take advantage of when opportunities arise.

Earnings Announcements

Quarterly earnings announcements are mandatory in many exchanges although jurisdictions like Hong Kong only require half-year earnings reports. Even so, some companies make voluntary quarterly earnings announcements when they are also listed on a secondary exchange.

Most companies that have ADRs traded in the United States (whether sponsored or unsponsored) are usually large enough in their home jurisdiction to warrant significant coverage by the investment community. This means that there will be analysts' earnings forecasts of the companies. When a company's earnings significantly exceed consensus analysts' estimates, which is a figure based on the combined estimates of analysts covering the company, the share price is expected to increase when trading resumes the following day. On the other hand, if the company missed estimates, the share price of the company is going to drop.

You should also note that beating or missing earnings estimates is just one aspect of earnings announcements. Of equal or sometimes greater importance can be the company guidance about upcoming sales or earnings estimates.

Comments by the company on its upcoming performance are typically enclosed in its earnings report made available to the stock exchanges and media. You should be able to identify whether there are opportunities to trade such stocks from this information.

Interpreting whether the earnings are beating or missing estimates can have a substantial effect on stock prices the next day and is most crucial. As earnings announcements occur regularly and predictably (in terms of the timing of the announcements), you can repeatedly take advantage of earnings surprises or shocks and trade the underlying ADRs accordingly to enjoy the information edge. Please refer to the case studies in later chapters to see how this can be done.

Government Policy Changes

In a country like China, where governmental policies have a large impact on the stock market, any changes in policies mean trading opportunities for savvy investors.

One such government policy that can impact share price is price control. Price control is implemented by the government mainly to control inflation or to protect domestic producers from foreign imports.

The Chinese government, through the National Development and Reform Commission (NDRC), controls the price of gasoline and diesel. The NDRC will adjust the price of these products based on a few factors including international price. The investment community has certain expectations on whether and when the price of gasoline and diesel will be adjusted. Many of the expectations will then be reflected in the share price of major oil and gas companies, such as Petro China and Sinopec. However, when an adjustment in price occurs unexpectedly, the share price of such companies are expected to reflect this sudden change in expectation. As illustrated in a later chapter, a savvy trade can actually make use of this kind of news about unexpected changes in gasoline-price adjustments and trade the ADRs of China oil companies profitably.

ENTERING THE MARKET

Now that you know what news causes prices to rise and you can locate the news, what else do you need to do before you can enter the market?

As explained earlier in this chapter, you have to know how to interpret such news. For earnings news, you need to be able to find out whether the figures released deviate significantly from the forecasts. Where can you find such consensus estimates?

ET Net Limited—Profit Estimation

ET Net Limited provides profit-estimate figures for companies listed on the Stock Exchange of Hong Kong, provided the companies are covered by major brokers. To get a profit estimate for Sinopec (00386. HK), for example, an investor just needs to go to www.etnet.com.hk and access the company's details by typing in the company stock code (00386) as shown in

FIGURE 3.12   ET Net Limited—Stock Quote
Source: ET Net Limited (www.etnet.com.hk).

Figures 3.12 (a stock quote screen) and 3.13 (a profit estimates screen with consensus estimations shown at the bottom of the page).

You must keep the current financial year's consensus profit estimations in mind and compare them against reported actual profit figures. If these two deviate substantially, there may be an opportunity to buy or sell the ADRs after Asian market hours.

Bloomberg Businessweek—Earnings and Estimates Summary

You can access the *Bloomberg Businessweek* website (investing.business week.com) to get information on a company's earnings estimates, including those listed in many exchanges worldwide.

In order to get the earnings estimates, you just key in the stock symbol of the company you wish to check and access the earnings tab on the company specific page.

As discussed in this chapter, you can find out when companies are expected to make earnings reports and how to compare actual earnings with consensus estimates using some of the website resources suggested. Nevertheless, simple comparisons as to whether the earnings reported exceed or miss street estimates may not be enough to assess the price impact the next day. You have to be able to look at the qualitative part of the financial results as well. (For more information on such qualitative analysis, see this book's Appendix.)

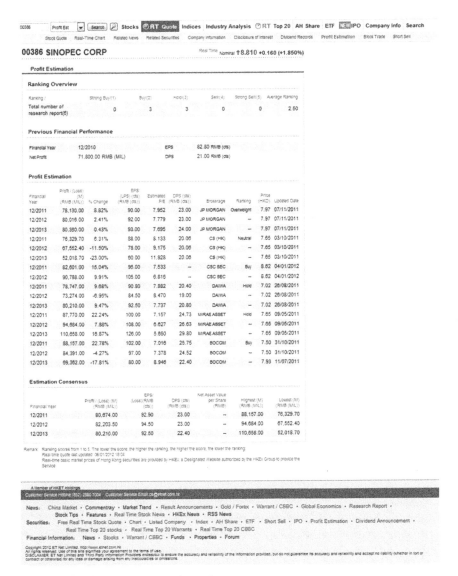

FIGURE 3.13 ET Net Limited—Profit Estimates

Source: ET Net Limited (www.etnet.com.hk).

SUMMARY

This chapter highlights the online resources you can rely on to look for price-sensitive news and information, particularly the underlying company's primary stock exchange official announcements page as the best starting point. Also covered are some of the financial news and investment websites in Asia that offer news relating to Asian ADRs that probably report first, as well as websites that offer price-moving announcements such as earnings reports.

However, after *finding* news that moves share prices, you must then know how to *interpret* it.

Chapter 4 discusses how we can set up brokerage accounts to start trading ADRs. It also looks at things to get equipped with before executing trades.

CHAPTER 4

Trading ADRs

I f you are now comfortable with the methods for gaining an edge in trading ADRs using the news and websites available to us, the next question you should ask is, "Where can I trade these ADRs?"

OPENING AN ACCOUNT

ADRs are listed in many exchanges and over-the-counter (OTC) markets in the United States, but the number of listings in OTC markets far exceed those in main exchanges like the NYSE and NASDAQ. Table 4.1 shows the number of ADRs listed in OTC market accounts for close to 70 percent of all ADRs. In order to trade effectively, we need to open accounts with stockbrokers with access to trading OTC market ADRs and also the ability to provide us with useful information.

TABLE 4.1 Number of ADRs Listed on Various Markets in the United States (as of January 11, 2012)

Name of Exchange/Market	Number of ADRs Listed
NASDAQ	105
NYSE	303
OTC	1930
OTCQX	36
PORTAL	433

Source: JP Morgan Chase & Co. (www.adr.com).

There are many stockbrokers, both U.S.-based and overseas, that investors can use to trade ADRs. As online trading and access to news through the Internet are essential for the implementation of the strategies in this book, we only highlight brokers here that have good online trading tools. For the benefit of international readers, we will also go through some regional brokers that offer ADRs trading.

U.S.-BASED BROKERS

Interactive Brokers (www.interactivebrokers.com)

Interactive Brokers offers online trading to many markets throughout the world from the United States to Hong Kong. Interactive Brokers provides electronic access to stocks, options, futures, foreign exchange products, bonds, and funds on over 100 market centers in 19 countries from one IB Universal Account. It is probably one of the best one-stop brokers in terms of market access because it enables you to trade OTC ADRs as well as foreign underlying stocks in one account. Interactive Brokers even support conversion of ADRs into foreign underlying shares.

Interactive Brokers also offers one of the cheapest brokerage rates around. Its website and trading tools are very useful to people who are frequent traders and have some knowledge of trading. Since Interactive Brokers' products include many exchanges worldwide, one useful tool is the ability to create stock charts with both the underlying share and its associated ADR at one glance.

Interactive Brokers may not be as useful for people who are not Internet savvy, because it deals with customers mainly through an assortment of online tools. If an investor prefers to speak to a live customer support officer when facing a problem, Interactive Brokers may not be the most suitable choice. Interactive Brokers' trading tools are useful to investors who know how to use them. Although they are a bit complicated, one might simply need to attend some of the webinars offered through their site to gain a better understanding of their tools.

Some of the most useful information investors can get from Interactive Brokers is in the form of the availability of stocks for shorting. This is very important when we would like to trade on the bad news of an ADR which does not have other derivatives, such as put options, for trading a stock down.

TD Ameritrade (www.tdameritrade.com)

TD Ameritrade is a leading online brokerage formed with the 2006 merger of Ameritrade and the brokerage division TD Waterhouse USA from TD

Bank Financial Group of Canada. The holding company, TD Ameritrade Holding Corporation, is listed on NASDAQ under the symbol AMTD.

TD Ameritrade is also home to the award-winning think-or-swim trading technology and the Investools investor education program. These tools are very useful for traders to analyze securities and options.

E*Trade (www.etrade.com)

E*Trade Financial Corporation is a stockbroker based in New York City that has operations in Europe and Asia besides its presence in the U.S. It is one of the global leaders in online trading. E*Trade offers trading of stocks, options, ADRs, ETFs, and fixed income securities. Besides U.S. securities, E*Trade also offers direct trading access to a few global stock markets including Hong Kong, Germany, Japan, Canada, and the United Kingdom.

International investors can choose to open their accounts in a country closest to them as E*Trade has offices in Europe, the Middle East, Singapore, and Hong Kong. It also offers multilingual customer services in 10 languages.

Charles Schwab (www.schwab.com)

The Charles Schwab Corporation is one of the largest financial services firms in the United States. It provides securities brokerage, banking, wealth management, and related financial services to investors worldwide through its subsidiaries, including Charles Schwab & Co. Inc., Charles Schwab Bank, and Charles Schwab, Hong Kong, Ltd.

Charles Schwab account holders enjoy multichannel access to ADR investing. This includes comprehensive ADR research resources, such as charts, reports, news, and analyst opinions, all of which can be accessed online.

Scottrade (www.scottrade.com)

Scottrade is a leading online brokerage firm that offers a full line of investment products, online trading, and market research tools to help investors take control of their financial future. It is a privately owned, American discount retail brokerage firm headquartered in St. Louis, Missouri. Scottrade also offers services to Asian-Pacific customers with a service center staffed with Chinese-speaking stockbrokers.

Scottrade also offers access to foreign stocks, providing customers the ability to trade international equities alongside domestic equities using one central account.

INTERNATIONAL BROKERS

Huatai Financial Holdings (www.htsc.com.hk)

Huatai Financial Holdings (Hong Kong) Limited is a wholly owned subsidiary of Huatai Securities Company Limited of China, one of the largest stockbrokers in China, and it is listed on the Shanghai Stock Exchange.

International investors who wish to have a better understanding of Chinese stocks may want to establish an account with Huatai Hong Kong through which they can also have access to trade U.S. ADRs.

Boom Securities (home.boom.com.hk)

Monex Boom Securities (H. K) Limited is a stockbroker based in Hong Kong which is wholly owned by Monex Group, one of the largest online financial services providers in Japan and listed on the Tokyo Stock Exchange. Monex Group also owns U.S.-based TradeStation Group and offers equities, options, futures, and forex trading.

For Asian investors, Boom offers access to securities listed in more than 10 countries using one single account.

Phillip Capital (www.poems.com.sg)

Established in 1975, Singapore-based Phillip Capital offers a full range of financial services to retail, corporate, and institutional customers. It operates in the financial hubs of 12 countries with offices in Singapore, Hong Kong, Malaysia, France, Australia, Sri Lanka, Thailand, Japan, Indonesia, the United Kingdom, China, and the United States.

Phillip offers Contract for Difference (CFD), a leverage-trading instrument, to investors. CFD is best suited for investors who want to benefit from the price movements of underlying shares, but do not need the rights to ownership.

CASH Financial Services (www.cashon-line.com)

CASH Financial Services Group is a financial services company listed on the Hong Kong Stock Exchange. The range of financial services it offers include international trading services for securities (HK, United States, and China B-shares), commodities, futures and options, mutual funds, bonds, equity-linked instruments (ELI) and principal-guaranteed notes (PGN), insurance, market research and analysis, wealth management and advisory services, asset management, investment banking, and institutional sales.

Investors can have trading access to global markets through a single trading account.

Ping An of China Securities (stock.pingan.com.hk)

Ping An of China Securities (Hong Kong) is the securities trading division of Ping An Insurance Group, one of the largest integrated financial services conglomerates in China.

Investors can trade global stocks and futures as well as accessing the latest research news on the Greater China equity market via its online trading platform.

GETTING THE EDGE

Now that we know what type of announcements and news can move share prices, we have to know how to take advantage of the situations to enjoy a free lunch in the stock market when opportunities arise. Once again, there are basically two categories of news that move prices:

1. Regular: News that you can expect will take place regularly, such as earnings announcements. In many jurisdictions, listed companies are required to disclose their quarterly earnings report. We can therefore look forward to earnings seasons to try to find such earnings surprises or shocks. Some companies do announce when they are going to release their earnings so we can plan to look for such announcements on the dates they are due.

2. Irregular: We cannot really plan to take advantage of irregular news but we can, of course, set alerts for news relating to stocks we monitor. However, in terms of irregular news, it is usually too late to take advantage of a news item when the alert reaches us because many other investors or traders have also received the same information.

Choosing ADRs to Monitor

There are hundreds of ADRs from the Greater China region in various markets in the United States. It is almost impossible for us to track each and every one of them. We must therefore choose a list of ADRs that we are comfortable with and wish to monitor closely. We should know these companies really well and be aware of the investment community's expectations for the companies' earnings.

When choosing ADRs to be included in your watch list, it is good to include quite a few not-so-popular names. The well-known names already have large followings and it is very likely that any news relating to prominent companies (such as PetroChina or China Mobile) would be broadcast by major news media with little delay.

It is also a good idea to have some unsponsored ADRs, where the underlying companies have no obligations to make any announcements to the authorities in the United States. Such companies' news is less likely to be carried by major news media soon after its release in the primary stock exchange.

Once you have decided on the ADRs that you wish to monitor, you should set up a watch list for them so you will be updated with relevant news when it's available.

You can use the tools provided from financial websites or your brokers to set up your list. Figure 4.1 illustrates an ADR watch list using tools provided by a prominent depository receipts issuer, BNY Mellon, which can be accessed at www.adrbnymellon.com/dr_watchlist.jsp.

Create your own personal watchlist to monitor trading activity and news for up to 50 DRs and/or indices.

To add a DR or index to your watchlist, enter a DR or index symbol, name or CUSIP:(Limit 50):　　　　　SUBMIT

Powered by Interactive Data Managed Solutions

CLICK ANY SECURITY NAME BELOW TO VIEW A COMPREHENSIVE PROFILE PAGE

As of 1/25/2012 10:26AM ET

Security Name	Symbol	CUSIP	Last	Chg	% Chg	Vol	News	Delete
» China Shenhua Energy Co Ltd	CSUAY	16942A302	45.65	+0.25	+0.55%	600		
» Tencent Hldgs Ltd	TCEHY	88032Q109	23.50	-0.13	-0.55%	28,570		
» Yanzhou Coal Mining Co Ltd	YZC	984846105	24.66	+0.06	+0.24%	26,889		
» Huaneng Power International Inc	HNP	443304100	23.75	-0.03	-0.13%	9,844		

DELETE SELECTED SECURITIES

Most Recent News Headlines for My DR Watchlist

» 11:53 AM ET Jan 24, 2012 : [HNP] Shares of HNP Up 27.5% Since Uptrend Call on Shares -

» 10:44 AM ET Jan 17, 2012 : [HNP] Shares of HNP Up 23.0% Since Uptrend Call on Shares -

» 10:06 AM ET Jan 10, 2012 : [HNP] Huaneng Power International Shares Up 21.7% Since SmarTrend's Buy Recommendation (HNP) -

» 8:25 AM ET Jan 10, 2012 : [HNP] Huaneng Power International, Inc. Power Generation Within China Increases by 22.03% in 2011 - PR Newswire

» 11:25 AM ET Dec 31, 2011 : [HNP] [YZC] Halter USX China Index Announces 2011 Year End and 4Q Results and Adds New Constituents - BusinessWire

» 7:32 PM ET Dec 26, 2011 : [HNP] JAPAN,TAIWAN, PROVINCE OF CHINA : Sumitomo to build Submarine Power Cable Project jointly with JPS - Al Bawaba Business

» 9:43 AM ET Dec 23, 2011 : [YZC] China's Yanzhou Coal Mining to buy Australia's Gloucester Coal - Al Bawaba Business

FIGURE 4.1　ADR Watch List

Source: BNY Mellon (www.adrbnymellon.com/dr_watchlist.jsp).

Get quotes

Name	Symbol	Last price	Change
Esprit Holdings Limited	330	10.1	-0.16
Yanzhou Coal Mining Co.	1171	12.3	-0.3
Sinopec Shanghai Petrochemical Co. Ltd.	338	2.33	0.01
Aluminum Corporation of China Limited	2600	3.33	-0.03

Portfolio related News

Esprit Reports Sharp Drop in Profit

Yanzhou Coal Completes Acquisition

China Coal Miners Surged on Extreme Weather

FIGURE 4.2 Sample ADR Portfolio Watch List
Source: Google Finance.

We can also utilize the My Portfolio section of web portals like Google or Yahoo! to create a list of securities to monitor. All news related to the securities in the portfolio will be displayed on the My Portfolio page. In order to capture news originating from the primary market, it is essential that the stock symbol is added to the portfolio for the underlying securities symbols from their primary exchange, as indicated by a sample ADR watch list in Figure 4.2.

The above watch list allows us to stay informed of any breaking news from sources referring to the primary exchange's listed underlying securities.

Finding Earnings News

Listed companies typically announce the date that they plan to release the company's earnings. Even if they do not announce the actual date of the earnings release, you can guess from the dates of previous years' announcements and the date of the board of directors' meeting to get a clue as to when to expect the earnings news. We can get an indication of when a particular company is expected to announce its earnings from an ADR issuer website, such as BNY Mellon. Figure 4.3 shows that the expected earnings release date of China Shenhua Energy Co. Ltd. will fall sometime between March 21 and 31.

We can then start to search for earnings announcements from the primary exchange announcements page on the expected dates we found from the ADRs issuer websites.

FIGURE 4.3 Estimated Earnings Release Date

Source: BNY Mellon (www.adrbnymellon.com).

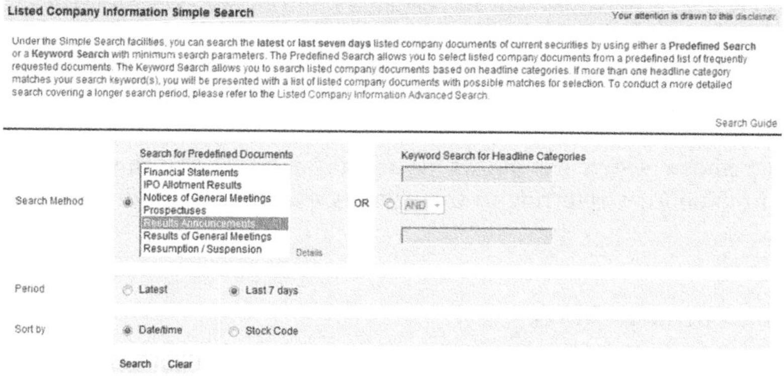

FIGURE 4.4 Searching for Results Announcements

Source: HKEx.

One way to keep close monitoring of earnings news is to search for all earnings announcements from primary exchanges on our list of ADRs. For example, since many of the ADRs you may monitor are listed on the Hong Kong Stock Exchange, it makes sense for us to do a search of result announcements on a daily basis during earnings seasons. Figure 4.4 illustrates how we can do this using the Simple Search section of the

Listed Company Information	Shareholding Disclosures	Issuer-related Information
· Latest Information	· Disclosure of Interests	· Prolonged Suspension Status Report
· Simple Search	· CCASS Shareholding Search	· Share Repurchases Reports
· Advanced Search		more ▶

Listed Company Information Simple Search - Predefined Search

From Date: 19/01/2012 To Date: 26/01/2012

Predefined Document: Results Announcements
(Delay in Results Announcement,Final Results,Interim Results,Quarterly Results)

Display records 1 to 4 (Total records found: 4)

Release Time	Code	Stock Name	Document
25/01/2012 18:06	06388	COACH-DRS-RS	Announcements and Notices - [Price-Sensitive Information / Quarterly Results] Announcement - Coach Reports Second Quarter Earnings (169KB, PDF)
19/01/2012 21:02	08169	ECO-TEK HLDGS	Announcements and Notices - [Final Results / Closure of Books or Change of Book Closure Period / Dividend or Distribution] FINAL RESULTS ANNOUNCEMENT FOR THE YEAR ENDED 31 OCTOBER 2011 (486KB, PDF)
19/01/2012 12:39	00010	HANG LUNG GROUP	Announcements and Notices - [Final Results / Dividend or Distribution / Closure of Books or Change of Book Closure Period] Results for the six months ended 31 December 2011 (220KB, PDF)
19/01/2012 12:31	00101	HANG LUNG PPT	Announcements and Notices - [Final Results / Dividend or Distribution / Closure of Books or Change of Book Closure Period] Results for the six months ended 31 December 2011 (223KB, PDF)

Search Again

FIGURE 4.5 Output of Earnings News Search
Source: HKEx.

HKExnews website. Figure 4.5 then shows the output of a search for Results Announcements from the HKExnews website.

Interpreting Earnings News

When companies announce a good set of results, it does not mean that the share price will go up. Share prices only move significantly when something unexpected happens. This means if a company announces earnings that beat or miss expectations by a significant margin, one can be reasonably sure that the share price will move up or down when trading resumes the next day.

In order to know whether the earnings discovered after Asian market hours are useful or not, we must be able to compare actual earnings against the estimated or forecasted earnings made by investment analysts through access to their consensus earnings estimates before we can decide whether a trading opportunity exists.

As indicated in Chapter 3, there are a couple of websites where we can find information on analysts' earnings estimates. But what is considered significant and what can we do to make sure we profit from such a trade?

Price Moves
There are three main things that can indicate a move in share prices in terms of earnings news.

1. When earnings reported exceed or miss consensus estimates by at least 20 percent.

   The 20 percent rule is a simple rule of thumb but the impact of the results will be more if the percentage deviation from analysts' estimates is more. The most useful scenario to act on would be when actual results are profits while analysts estimate a loss or when a company is reporting losses when analysts are expecting profits.

   However, we cannot just look at earnings at the superficial level. We have to look at earnings figures in detail to ensure a better interpretation of their results. For example, we have to make sure that the earnings deviation from analysts' estimates is due entirely to operating profit and not because of unusual or extraordinary items.

2. When the price of the underlying shares or ADRs have not moved up substantially enough.

   Company share prices may move up or down on days leading to the release of a company's earnings report. This is usually due to traders trying to take positions ahead of the news. When this happens, the share price may have already made its big move ahead of the actual results being released. This means that price impacts from earnings surprises or shocks may be mitigated once the results are released.

   You must therefore analyze the price movement ahead of the earnings announcement. It is easier to act when a price has not moved much ahead but if it has already moved, you must then make a decision whether the actual figure is big enough to enhance the price movement or not. This requires some experience and market feel. If we are not sure of such impact, it is better to avoid trading to avoid possible losses.

3. When management releases commentary on future prospects.

   Management's commentary on a company's prospects in the future may be even more significant price movers than the actual earnings. Management normally discusses the company's future outlook in its earnings report note.

   You can expect price movements when management makes comments that deviate substantially from their current trend. For example, a company may have suffered losses for eight consecutive quarters and had not made any statement in the past indicating a change in earnings trends. But when management starts making positive comments on upcoming quarters or financial years, indicating a change in earnings trends, share prices are then expected to move.

There are a few more things to consider when interpreting a company's financial results:

1. Breaking down the analysis of earnings to the latest period under reporting.

   This means that if a quarterly earnings report is released, you should be looking at the latest quarter to compare with previously reported quarters and also whether there is a slowdown in growth momentum (a negative sign) or a recovery in losses (a positive sign).

   A company may report a sharp drop in profit compared with the corresponding period from the last financial year, but such a drop may be an improvement compared to the immediate past quarter. If there is no seasonal pattern, such developments may be viewed positively and be positive for the share price.

2. Looking at the core earnings figure instead of the final earning number.

   This is because there may be other items that contributed to the profit of the company but such items may not be viewed as recurring. Accounting profit due to gains in the foreign exchange or market value of securities also may not be viewed as sustainable and hence have limited impact on share price. Investors must also exercise extraordinary care analyzing real estate stocks, as profit may be due substantially to property revaluation.

3. Checking if they set operating targets.

   Some companies do set operating targets like revenue, operating margins, and so on, and disclose them in their financial reports. It is useful to assess whether companies have managed to achieve targets set in the previous financial periods.

   Companies that consistently beat their targets may be accorded a premium rating by the investment community.

4. Paying attention to new products and services or new business segments when analyzing a company's results.

   Past profits are just historical figures. It is the future prospects that are most important. For example, a mobile phone manufacturer may see growth in a new market segment like smartphones with higher margin as opposed to declining sales in normal phones. Such information disclosed in a company's financial reports may indicate better prospects for the company moving forward and may impact the share price positively.

5. Analyzing production costs and sales margins.

   Doing these exercises may give further insight into a company's financial position.

HEEDING POSITIVE PROFIT ALERTS OR NEGATIVE PROFIT WARNINGS

Many companies issue positive profit alerts or profit warnings when their upcoming earnings will deviate substantially relative to the previous corresponding period. When profit alerts are issued and such factors have not been taken into consideration by the analysts' community, the share price can be expected to move up or down significantly.

However, if such profit deviations are already accounted for in an analysts' consensus forecast, the impact of the resulting share price is not expected to be significant.

Since announcements of profit alerts are not a regular event, there is no way we can plan for their impact on specific ADRs. However, you can choose to be hard working and search for all profit alerts that have been announced on all companies listed in the exchanges of the ADRs you monitor.

For example, you can search for all the latest announcements containing the keyword "profit alert" in the news title using the Advanced Search feature of the HKExnews website to scan for companies that have released profit alerts on any given day, as illustrated following Figures 4.6 and 4.7.

After we obtain a list of the companies issuing profit alerts on a particular day, you can check if such companies have any ADRs being traded in the United States.

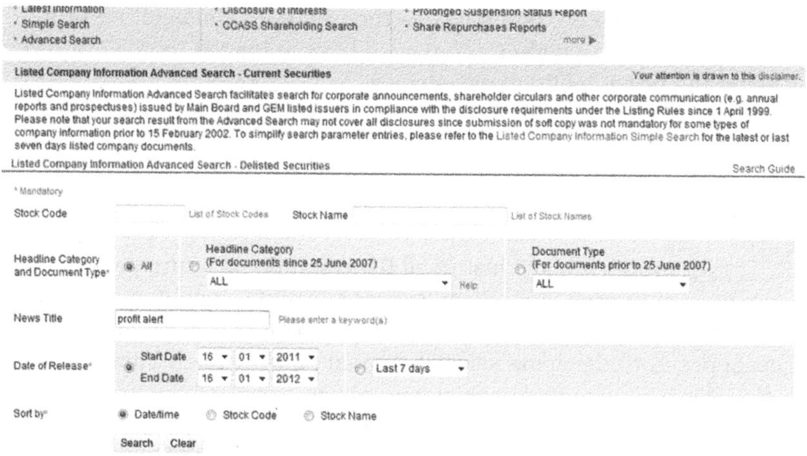

FIGURE 4.6　Search for Profit Alert

Source: HKEx.

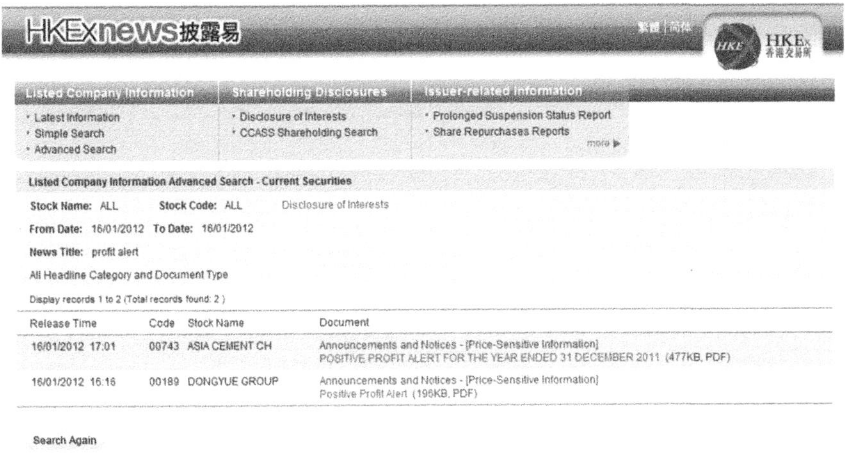

FIGURE 4.7 Results for Profit Alert

Source: HKEx.

In the search result of Figures 4.6 and 4.7, the companies who issued profit alerts on those particular days are Asia Cement China and Dongyue Group. When you search for the companies' ADRs from BNY Mellon ADR database, they appear to have ADRs traded under the symbols AACEY and DNGYY. However when you search for such securities in our broker's trading system, the securities have no bid and ask price and may not even be tradable under most brokers.

On closer examination, you can find these two ADRs listed under the Grey Market of the OTC Market.

Although the ADRs of the above companies are available, they are not quoted or traded on an exchange or interdealer quotation system. Broker-dealers report trades in grey market stocks to their Self Regulatory Organization (SRO) and the SRO then distributes the trade data to various market data vendors and financial websites so investors can track price and volume. Because of such restrictions, we cannot trade Grey Market ADRs effectively.

EXECUTING ADR TRADES

After you find news that you believe will allow you to trade an ADR profitably, you should compare the ADR price against the underlying security's price in the primary exchange to determine if you are entering the trade at an advantageous price.

FIGURE 4.8   Guangshen Railway ADR
Source: BNY Mellon (www.adrbnymellon.com).

In order to arrive at an approximate price of an ADR that reflects the primary exchange's last traded price, you should know what the ADR exchange ratio is and the foreign exchange rate of the currency where the underlying security is quoted. See Figure 4.8 for an example using Guangshen Railway's ADR.

The last traded price of Guangshen Railway (00525. HK) in Hong Kong was HKD2.80. In order to approximate the ADR (GSH) price, you need to multiply the ADR ratio of 50 and adjust for the exchange rate between Hong Kong dollars and U.S.dollars as follows:

Guangshen Railway Hong Kong Price = HKD2.80 (January 27, 2012)
Calculated Guangshen Railway ADR (GSH) Price
= (2.80 * 50)/7.75
= USD18.06

On some websites, you may be able to get the prices of both the underlying shares in the primary market and the corresponding ADR prices on the same page. See Figure 4.9 which shows a screenshot from www. AASTOCKS.com with both the Hong Kong's underlying share price and the corresponding U.S. ADR's price together with the exchange ratio and conversion premium/discount.

After you have found the ADR price, you should then compare whether the premium or discount of the ADR against its Hong Kong underlying share price is within normal range. You can assume an ADR premium or discount of less than two percent after adjusting for trading-day market bias as a reasonable range. If this is the case, it means that the ADR price reflects the closing price of the security in Hong Kong. You may also factor in the movement in the United States (a broader market) to reflect an expected upward or downward bias of prices in the home exchange the next day.

If you believe the news you obtain has the potential to move the underlying share price by at least 5 percent the next day in the primary exchange and the ADR price only reflects the closing price in the primary exchange plus some broader market bias, then you can safely execute a trade with the hope that a profit can be made the next day.

When the underlying security does, in fact, make the move you expected the next day, you should be able to close your position at the open of the U.S. market as traders and market makers adjust the ADR price.

SHORT SELLING ADRS

When you come across a piece of negative news for the ADR you are monitoring, you will want to short the security.

It would be best if the ADR you want to short is an optionable stock so you can easily buy a put or short a call depending on your interpretation of the magnitude of the bad news and its effect on the share price. Otherwise, you have to short sell the ADR. Before you can be comfortable entering into a short trade, however, you should understand the mechanics of short selling.

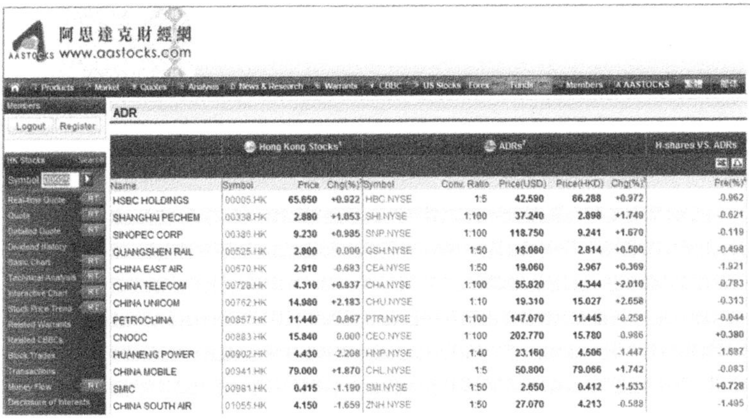

Name	Symbol	Price	Chg(%)	Symbol	Conv. Ratio	Price(USD)	Price(HKD)	Chg(%)	Pre(%)
HSBC HOLDINGS	00005.HK	65.650	+0.922	HBC.NYSE	1:5	42.590	66.288	+0.972	-0.962
SHANGHAI PECHEM	00338.HK	2.880	+1.853	SHI.NYSE	1:100	37.240	2.898	+1.749	-0.621
SINOPEC CORP	00386.HK	9.230	+0.985	SNP.NYSE	1:100	118.750	9.241	+1.670	-0.119
GUANGSHEN RAIL	00525.HK	2.800	0.000	GSH.NYSE	1:50	18.080	2.814	+0.500	-0.498
CHINA EAST AIR	00670.HK	2.910	-0.683	CEA.NYSE	1:50	19.060	2.967	+0.369	-1.921
CHINA TELECOM	00728.HK	4.310	+0.937	CHA.NYSE	1:100	55.820	4.344	+2.010	-0.783
CHINA UNICOM	00762.HK	14.980	+2.183	CHU.NYSE	1:10	19.310	15.027	+2.658	-0.313
PETROCHINA	00857.HK	11.440	-0.867	PTR.NYSE	1:100	147.070	11.445	-0.258	-0.044
CNOOC	00883.HK	15.840	0.000	CEO.NYSE	1:100	202.770	15.780	-0.986	+0.380
HUANENG POWER	00902.HK	4.430	-2.208	HNP.NYSE	1:40	23.160	4.506	-1.447	-1.687
CHINA MOBILE	00941.HK	79.000	+1.870	CHL.NYSE	1:5	50.800	79.066	+1.742	-0.083
SMIC	00981.HK	0.415	-1.190	SMI.NYSE	1:50	2.650	0.412	+1.533	+0.728
CHINA SOUTH AIR	01055.HK	4.150	-1.659	ZNH.NYSE	1:50	27.070	4.213	-0.588	-1.495

FIGURE 4.9 Hong Kong Share versus ADR Price
Source: AASTOCKS.com Limited.

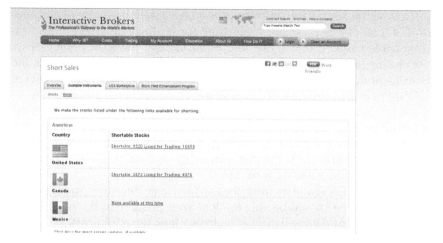

FIGURE 4.10   Stocks Available for Shorting as of January 15, 2012
Source: Interactive Brokers LLC.

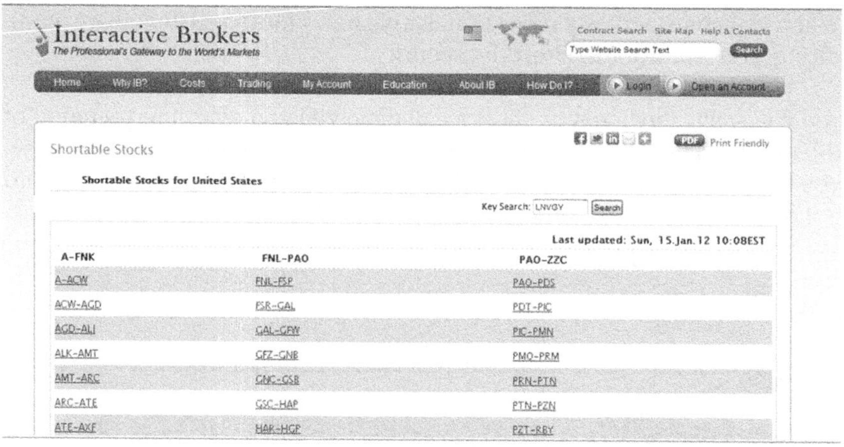

FIGURE 4.11   Entering Specific Stocks to Check Short Availability
Source: Interactive Brokers.

Selling short means a trader is selling a security that he or she does not own. More specifically, a short sale is the sale of a security that isn't owned by the seller, but is promised for delivery.

When you short sell a stock, you must first confirm that you are able to borrow the stock you plan to short sell. Stockbrokers will normally keep a list of the available inventory of stocks for short sale. The inventory comes

FIGURE 4.12 Query Results for Number of Shares Available for Shorting

Source: Interactive Brokers LLC.

from the broker's own shares, shares of others (including its customers who borrow on margin and agree to lend their shares), and other third-party brokers.

When the borrowed shares are sold, the broker will use the shares in their inventory to settle the short sale and the proceeds from the sale are credited to the brokerage account. The cash received from selling the shares is then used as collateral on the borrowed shares.

If the share price drops as you expected, you would close your profitable short position by buying back the same number of shares and returning them to your broker. However, if the share price rises, you have to buy it back at the higher price and lose money.

Stockbrokers such as Interactive Brokers make it easy for their customers to be able to determine whether the security they wish to short is available and in what quantity. Figures 4.10, 4.11, and 4.12 illustrate how Interactive Brokers' customers can search for stocks to sell short (using Lenovo, or LNVGY, as an example) at a particular point in time.

Note that after you enter the stock symbol LNVGY and click search, you will arrive at page showing the stock symbol and name. Once there, press Check Availability to arrive at the number of shares available to short (1,000 in the case in Figure 4.12).

SUMMARY

As you equip yourself with the knowledge to gain an edge in trading ADRs, you must also be able to find a good stockbroker to execute your trade.

In today's fast-moving market environment, the ability to trade online in an uninterrupted manner is important to take advantage of price discrepancies that may only be valid for a short period of time.

With so many ADRs listed on OTC Markets, you must also have access to brokers that allow you to buy and sell OTC-listed securities. For readers residing outside of the United States, there are many alternatives in terms of Asian brokers who may be able to help you interpret after-hours news. In Asia, however, you may need to look for a full-service broker, rather than a discount online broker, so you do not misinterpret the news.

You should also find out how to short sell ADRs when you discover negative news coming out of Asia on specific companies. Chapter 5 discusses some of the instruments available to help you short ADRs more effectively. Otherwise, you will have to find out from your broker whether the ADRs you want to short sell are shortable and in what amount.

After learning the tricks to make money, how do we enhance our profits? The next chapter introduces the concept of leverage and looks at some instruments to use to achieve greater gain.

CHAPTER 5

Using Leverage Instruments to Enhance Return

A fter doing the necessary research and discovering news that can lead you to an almost risk-free profit overnight, you are probably very excited about making money on a particular trade. However, historical results suggest that you can only expect an overnight gain of between 3 to 5 percent. While most investors would be happy with 3 to 5 percent return per annum, many traders would not be too excited with such percentage returns, even for short-term trading.

In order to enhance return on your almost risk-free trade, you may use leverage instruments to achieve the desired return. In this chapter, we look at a few types of leverage instruments that can enhance your return. Traders should also be aware that although the use of leverage instruments creates an opportunity for increased returns on targeted securities, it also carries increased risks and can magnify your losses if your expectation turns out to be incorrect.

In the equity world, the most common leverage instrument is the call or put option. Nevertheless, not all ADRs have exchange-traded options as most ADRs are not listed on big exchanges that attract big enough followings for options exchanges to list them. Besides options, international traders can consider contract for difference (CFD). CFDs on equities are not allowed in many jurisdictions due to possible rivalries with local stock exchanges. We may have to open CFD accounts in countries like Australia or Singapore in order to be able to trade CFDs on equity worldwide. Also, single-stock futures is another type of leverage instrument that some traders can consider where it is available.

USING OPTIONS TO ENHANCE RETURN

An option is a derivative instrument that entitles the holder to the right (not the obligation) to buy or sell the underlying security at a predetermined price known as the strike price (or exercise price) on or before a predetermined date known as the expiration date. The underlying security can be a share, an ADR, a basket of shares, a share index, a foreign currency, or virtually any type of traded security.

A call option entitles the holder to buy the underlying securities at the strike price on or before expiration date. A put option, on the other hand, allows the holder to sell the underlying securities at the strike price on or before the expiration date.

Figure 5.1 illustrates the cash payoff of a call option at an expiration date.

For a call option, the investor pays a price (or premium) for owning it. If at the expiration date, the price of the underlying share is higher than the strike price, the investor will exercise the call option. The difference between the market price of the underlying share and the strike price is the gross profit on the option investment. Net profit is arrived after deducting the price paid for the option and associated trading costs from the gross profit. However, if the price of the underlying share is below the exercise price, the option will expire worthless. When we buy call

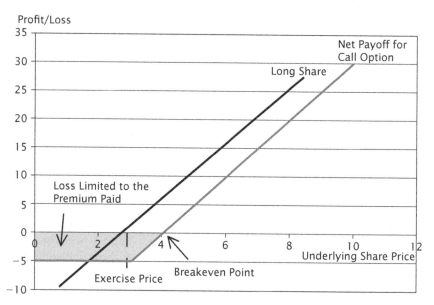

FIGURE 5.1 Call Option Payoff

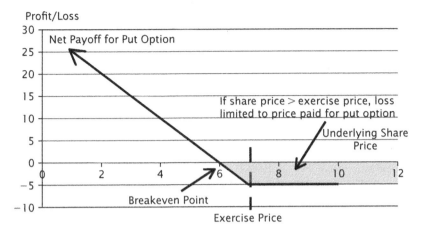

FIGURE 5.2　Put Option Payoff

options, our maximum loss is limited to the price (premium) we paid for the options.

For a put option, the situation is the opposite. If the price of the underlying share is below the strike price on expiration, the investor will exercise the put option and sell the share at the strike price, claiming the difference between the market price and the strike price as the gross profit. If the price of the underlying share is above that of the strike price, the put option would not be exercised. Figure 5.2 illustrates the payoff of a put option on the expiration date.

FACTORS AFFECTING THE PRICE OF OPTIONS

The price of options is determined by a number of factors including:

- The price of the underlying security
- Strike price
- Time to expiration
- The volatility of underlying security
- Interest rate
- Dividend rate

Table 5.1 illustrates the impact of various factors on the price of call and put options.

TABLE 5.1   Factors Affecting Options Price

When the Following Increases . . .	Impact on Call Option Price	Impact on Put Option Price
Underlying Price	↑	↓
Strike Price	↓	↑
Time to Expiration	↑	↑
Volatility of Underlying Security	↑	↑
Interest Rate	↑	↓
Dividend Rate	↓	↑

Underlying Price

As an option is a derivative from the underlying security, there is a direct relationship between the underlying price and the price of the option.

For a call option, the relationship between underlying security price and option price is positive. When the security price rises, the greater the chance is that the option would be exercised and therefore the call option price increases.

For a put option, the situation is reversed. When the underlying security price increases, there is less of a chance the put options get exercised and hence the price of the put option drops.

Strike Price

The strike price of a call option has an inverse relationship with the price of the latter. The higher the strike price, the lower the price of the option as option holders will need to pay more to exercise the option.

In the case of a put option, the option holder will need to pay more to exercise the option as the strike price gets higher.

Time to Expiration

The value of an option, in theory, can be divided into two parts:

1. Intrinsic Value
2. Time Value

Or, in other words, when represented as an equation, as follows:
$$\text{Option Price} = \text{Intrinsic Value} + \text{Time Value}$$

Time value is the value attached to the time left to maturity. An option that has 12 months left before expiration is worth more than an option that has only 2 months left because a 12-month option offers the option holder a greater chance for the underlying of moving in-the-money. Effectively, time value represents the speculative value of the option that the investor pays to benefit from a favorable change in the price of the underlying, during the life of the option. As the option moves closer to expiration, the time value also decreases.

Volatility of the Underlying Security

An important element affecting the price of an option is the volatility of the underlying security. Volatility represents the price movements, both up and down, in the underlying security over a period of time. The more volatile the underlying, the greater the potential profits from the option. High volatility indicates that the underlying asset price varies sharply (both up and down) and could exceed investor expectations. Thus, both call and put options prices benefit from higher volatility.

There are two types of volatility:

1. **Historical volatility**, which is calculated using past variations in the price of the underlying. Past variations give some idea of the potential for future variations.
2. **Implied volatility,** which represents market expectations of future volatility in the price of the underlying stock.

Interest Rate

Buying call options can be seen as buying the underlying securities on margin as the option buyer only comes up with a fraction of the cost of buying the underlying security. Therefore, when the interest rate rises, the value of the call option should rise to reflect the "higher cost of financing" to purchase the underlying security.

In the case of put options, a sale of the underlying security may take place at expiration. The situation is therefore the reverse: the higher the interest rate, the lower the put option price. If you sell the underlying security first rather than buying a put option, you would have been able to invest the proceeds from the sale in the money market and would have received interest income. Thus, if the interest rate is higher, you would receive more in interest income and hence the price of the put option should be lower.

Dividend Rate

The underlying security's dividend rate will affect the price of the option. The option holder is not entitled to any dividend payment unless she or he exercises the option prior to the entitlement date of the dividend. As option holders are not expected to exercise the option prior to expiration in a perfect market, expectations of a higher dividend rate will have a negative impact on the price of an option.

For a put option, higher dividends add to the attractiveness of the option because the security price would be adjusted downwards in a bigger magnitude when it goes ex-dividend, adding to the value of the put.

CHOOSING WHICH OPTION TO BUY

Options on securities are traded in exchanges such as the Chicago Board Options Exchange (CBOE). Not all securities have stock options that can be traded. The exchange will decide what underlying securities are included in its equities options list.

If after you have done your analysis you decided that Company A's share price should rise the next day and its ADR price has barely moved in the U.S. market, you can choose to trade on its ADR's call options if you want to enhance the return of our trade. However, how do you know which strike price you should buy?

For example, call options with a March expiration for Company A. Company A's ADR price was trading at US$50.40 on February 7. Table 5.2 includes indicative prices of a series of Company A's March ADR call options and their respective prices.

Company A announced a sharp jump in net profit of 20 percent, beating the consensus analysts' estimate that only projected a 5 percent rise in net profit, after market hours in Asia on February 7.

Based on the information above, Company A's price will surge 5 percent when the market resumes trading the next day. Since, Company A's ADR price has barely moved, buying Company A's ADR will allow you to take a position ahead of price movement and profit from it when the underlying share price does indeed move up the next day.

If you think the ADR price will fully reflect the expected 5 percent underlying share price move, you can buy the ADR at US$50.40. You need

TABLE 5.2 Call Options of Company A with March Expiration

Strike	Bid	Ask	Last
45.00	5.30	5.50	5.40
47.50	3.20	3.40	3.80
50.00	1.45	1.55	1.65
52.50	0.45	0.55	0.45

to come up with US$50,400 to buy 1,000 ADRs of Company A assuming you are using a fully cash funded brokerage account. If the next day, Company A's ADR moves up about 5 percent to US$53.00, you would make a gross profit of about US$2,600 before commission charges. This represents a gross trading gain of 5 percent.

However, if you buy into Company A's ADR call option with a strike price of US$45 at the ask price of US$5.50, you can expect to make a profit of at least 45 percent based on the intrinsic value of US$8 for the call option when the ADR price reaches US$53. The ask price is used because market makers change the bid-ask price for options continuously and the last traded price may not be reflective of the current market price of the underlying share.

Sounds good, right? But it can be better!

If you buy into Company A's ADR call option with a strike price of US$47.50 at the ask price of US$3.40, the potential gain can be over 61 percent based on the intrinsic value of US$5.50 when the ADR price moves to US$53. If you only use intrinsic value (to be on the safe side) to project call option prices, you could potentially make over 93 percent if you bought the US$50 strike call option.

But the best profit is usually made when you buy an at-the-money call option or slightly out-of-the-money call option. If the ADR price moves above the strike price of an out-of-the-money call option, the percentage return can be the highest. However, due to the complexity of such a trade and the associated higher risk, such a position may not suit the novice trader.

In the example of Company A's ADR, you should choose the at-the-money call option (strike price US$50) to optimize our gain. You do not come across such earnings surprises to the upside very often. When it takes place, you must be ready to make a killing, and buying an at-the-money call option gives you a very good chance to achieve that.

On the flip side, if the underlying company releases bad news such as a profit warning, you should take advantage of the situation and leverage by buying a put option.

Using the previous example on Company A's ADR, let's now look at the put options. Table 5.3 shows indicative prices of a series of March Company A's ADR put options and their respective prices.

Let us assume that Company A now issues a profit warning saying that the company will suffer a 30 percent drop in net profit against market expectation of a rise in profit, after market hours in Asia on February 7.

Based on the information provided, you believe that the share price should drop 10 percent from the last traded price. You again come across a situation where the ADR of Company A barely moved at the U.S. trading hour.

TABLE 5.3 Put Options of Company A with March Expiration

Strike	Bid	Ask	Last
45.00	0.05	0.15	0.10
47.50	0.30	0.40	0.30
50.00	0.95	1.10	1.08
52.50	2.45	2.60	2.50

To increase your potential trading gain, you would purchase a put option of Company A's ADR. As you are expecting a big drop in share price the next day, you may want to be more aggressive and choose a put option that is out-of-the-money.

If you choose the put option with a strike price of US$47.50 and bought it at the ask price of US$0.40, the option price can be expected to increase to US$2.50 based on intrinsic value alone if the ADR price plunges 10 percent to about US$45.00 the next trading day. This represents a gain of about 525 percent over one night. You may even make more in percentage terms had you chosen the put option with a strike price of US$45.00 but that involves more complicated calculations using option Greeks (which is outside the scope of this book).

Even if you want to be conservative and choose to buy the at-the-money put option of US$50 strike price at US$1.10, you should still make a very good profit of 350 percent based on the intrinsic value of the put option at US$5.00 when the ADR price drops to US$45.00.

In short, you can make triple-digit percentage gains on material information released after Asian market hours if you know how to interpret them and use call or put options to magnify your gains.

CONTRACT FOR DIFFERENCE

Contract for difference (or CFD) is a trading instrument that allows you to participate in the price movement of an underlying share with a fraction of the cost of buying or shorting the full share. This product is popular in the United Kingdom, Australia, Singapore, and some other Asian jurisdictions. CFDs on individual shares may not be available in many jurisdictions due to legal restrictions although investors worldwide can always choose to open their CFD trading account in jurisdictions that allow such products, like Singapore and Australia. CFDs are somewhat similar to margin financing and may expire at a predefined date (say, every month's end). Some over-the-counter products can be rolled over for a fee. But many CFD providers now no longer charge roll over fees due to increased competition.

A major benefit of trading CFDs is the ability of the investors to trade on a small margin. This means that investors can trade a full portfolio of shares (including some ADRs), indices, or commodities without having to tie up large amounts of capital. For example, investors may only need to come up with a margin deposit as low as 2 percent of the cost of buying the underlying share when trading CFDs. This margin requirement varies depending on the CFD providers and the type of securities that are traded.

As with all margin products, there is a financing charge incurred on long CFD positions. The financing charge is dependent on the underlying currency on which the securities are quoted. Financing charges are incurred because you must only pay a fraction of the cost of buying securities (usually 10 percent) through the CFD and borrow the rest of the capital. If you only come up with US$1,000 to buy a stock worth US$10,000, you are effectively borrowing US$9,000 or the difference between the cost of buying the stock and the deposit that you pay. If we purchase a stock that is quoted on high-yield currency like the Australian dollar, our cost of borrowing (or the financing charges) when buying CFDs would be relatively higher compared with buying a stock quoted in a lower yielding currency like the U.S.dollar. The financing charge is usually quoted at a premium of a couple of hundred basis points above the interbank rate quoted in a particular currency.

When you enter into a short CFD trade, there is a possibility that you can actually earn interest or incur negative financing charges because you may earn interest on your short-sale proceeds less the borrowing cost of the securities you shorted. However, whether you actually earn any interest will depend on the underlying currency the stock is quoted on.

When opening a short position, you receive cash payment for the full value of your short position and receive interest on this amount at the interbank rate less, say, 200 basis points per annum. If the interbank rate of currency A is 5 percent, you may earn 3 percent in interest (5 percent less 200 basis points or 2 percent) before deducting the borrowing cost of the shares. And if the borrowing cost of the share is 1 percent, you will earn a net interest of 2 percent per annum. For CFD trading purposes, the financing charge or credit is accrued on a daily basis. The overnight interest rate is usually calculated by dividing the per annum applicable interest rate payable by 365 (days per year).

There are a number of CFD providers that offer U.S. stocks (including ADRs) as products for CFD trading. Depending on the individual provider's offerings, traders can typically trade U.S. equity CFDs by putting in a margin deposit of 10 to 25 percent.

TABLE 5.4 CFD Long Position

Opening Long Company A's ADR Position	CFD Deal
Price	US$50.40
CFDs bought for US$5,040 exposure	1,000 shares
Total Exposure	US$50,400
Commission (say 0.10%)	US$50.40
Margin Requirement (10%)	US$5,040
Initial Outlay	US$5,090.40

Closing Long Company A's ADR Position	CFD Deal
Price	US$53.00
CFDs Sold to Close Position	1,000 shares
Position Size Closed	US$53,000
Commission (say 0.10%)	US$53.00
Financing Charge at 3.5% Per Annum/365	US$4.83
Gross Profit	**US$2,600**
Net Profit (Gross Profit–Trading Cost–Financing Charge)	**US$2,491.77**
Return on US$5,040 deposit	**49.4%**

Let us revisit the example we have on Company A's ADR and see how the return can be enhanced using CFDs. In our previous example of earnings surprises, Company A's ADR price was expected to rise from US$50.40 to US$53.00. If you had used a CFD to trade 1,000 shares of Company A's ADR on the long side, you only would have to come up with 10 percent of US$50,400 (or US$5,040).

If the ADR rises 5 percent the next day to US$53.00 as expected, you could make a gross profit of US$2,600. As you only need to come up with US$5,040 with a CFD, the percentage return becomes a highly attractive 51 percent.

However, you do incur commission charges for trading and financing charges for going long on a CFD trade even if it is for one day. Therefore, your net return of investment for this CFD trade is actually 49.4 percent as illustrated in Table 5.4.

In the example of earnings shocks when you expect Company A's share price to drop 10 percent, you can similarly utilize a CFD to short Company A's ADR and benefit from the expected price decline. Since you only come up with a 10 percent margin, your profit from selling the ADR at US$50.40 and closing the position at US$45.00 will provide you with 105.2 percent overnight gain, as illustrated in Table 5.5.

TABLE 5.5 CFD Short Position

Opening Short Company A's ADR Position	CFD Deal
Price	US$50.40
CFDs Sold for US$5,040 Exposure	1,000 shares
Total Exposure	US$50,400
Commission (say 0.10%)	US$50.40
Margin Requirement (10%)	US$5,040
Initial Outlay	US$5,090.40

Closing Short Company A's ADR Position	CFD Deal
Price	US$45.00
CFDs Bought to Close Position	1,000 shares
Position size closed	US$45,000
Commission (say 0.10%)	US$45.00
Financing Charge is Assumed to be 0% as We May Not Receive Any Financing Credit Due to Low Interest Rate	
Gross Profit	**US$5,400**
Net Profit (Gross Profit–Trading Cost)	**US$5,304.60**
Return on US$5,040 deposit	**105.2%**

SINGLE-STOCK FUTURES

Single-stock futures are futures contracts on specific stocks (including many ADRs) that expire and deliver stocks that coincide with the securities options market's expiration dates. Single-stock futures in the United States are traded on the OneChicago equity finance exchange. OneChicago trades are cleared at the Options Clearing Corporation, which functions as a central counterparty to each trade participant.

In order to trade single-stock futures, we are subject to a minimum of a 20 percent initial and maintenance margin requirement. Single-stock futures use mark-to-market accounting. This means that the single-stock futures are revalued daily at current market prices. After a single-stock futures position has been established, the clearinghouse will collect from the short (seller of single-stock futures) and pay to the long (buyer of single-stock futures) on each trading day when the underlying stock goes up. When the stock goes down, the clearinghouse will collect from the long and pay to the short. Upon liquidation of the contract, you will be credited for gains and debited for losses.

On expiration day, the short delivers to the long 100 shares for each long contract (similar to when a call option is exercised and the seller of the short call option must deliver 100 shares to the holder of the call). The stockbroker does these deliveries automatically. If you are on the short side and do not have the shares in your account, you will become short the shares.

Even though single-stocks futures offer you exposure to trading, it may not be as useful as a CFD as its bid-ask spread tends to be wider than those of normal stock quotes. Since most CFD brokers offer bid-ask rates based on underlying securities quotes, using single-stocks futures for trading ADRs may not provide any superior effect.

SUMMARY

In this chapter, we have reviewed three products that can give you leverage exposure to the underlying stocks or ADRs which you plan to trade. These products are not available on many ADRs, especially those listed over-the-counter. You can therefore only use leverage when options, CFDs, or single-stock futures are available for the ADRs you want to enter a position in.

In order to be able to take advantage of leverage when the opportunities arise, it is a good idea to open trading accounts with stockbrokers that allow you access to options trading, CFDs, and single-stock futures. Most of the larger U.S. stockbrokers should be able to provide their clients access to equity options and single-stock futures. CFD accounts that allow equity trading are actually not available in many jurisdictions due to legal restrictions and are therefore an option only for international traders who do not mind making an effort to establish a CFD account directly in the jurisdictions that allow such products.

You can achieve highest leverage with out-of-the-money options. If you are very sure of the price impact of the news and the magnitude of price movement, out-of-the-money options should provide you with the highest return. Alternatively, you can also try your luck with out-of-the-money options if you are not too sure of the price impact because the investment outlay is relatively small but you must control your position carefully because it is quite easy for you to suffer substantial losses with out-of-the-money options if the magnitude of the share price movement misses your expectation.

After getting excited with leveraged returns, one should be wary of potential risks when the supposedly good or bad news turns out to be not so good or bad enough for the share price to react. In the next chapter, we discuss what can go wrong when traders are not careful in using news to trade ADRs.

CHAPTER 6

What Could Go Wrong?

U p until this point, we have assumed making money using after-hours Asian trading news or announcements to trade U.S.-listed ADRs is almost a sure bet, but is that really so? Is the free lunch for real?

Frankly speaking, if you have done your homework thoroughly and understand how to interpret earnings (including the correct reading of financial statements), there is really very little margin for error. However, as a prudent investor or trader, you must also be aware of possible pitfalls that can cost you if you are not careful.

WHAT TO LOOK FOR IN AN EARNINGS REPORT

Regarding the release of a company's financial results, you need to know what to look for in order to buy the company's share at the post-earnings report stage. You also need to know what will cause the buying momentum during that post-earnings release stage to increase or decline. The following pages outline four situations to look for.

Earnings that Beat Expectations

This is one of the most obvious reasons why investors buy a company's shares. Even when a company announces a sharp drop in earnings, as long as the drop is much less than expected, investors will buy them. Traders who had shorted the stock would also need to cover their positions.

It is actually safer to trade on earnings surprises when the market has already discounted the expected poor performance of a company's results, such as a sharp drop in earnings. This is because such news would catch everyone, especially the short sellers, off guard and lead to panic buying or short covering.

When a company announces earnings that are better than expected on the positive growth side—say, a profit growth of 20 percent versus an expectation of 10 percent—the price impact may not be as strong as a turnaround case. If such earnings surprises occur on a day when the market in general is doing badly, you may not get the price impact you desire. One reason that may explain a lack of further momentum would be an absence or lack of short sellers to build up positions ahead of earnings.

Generally, you should have more short positions built up, ready to pounce on poor earnings, rather than short positions built up to take advantage of the possibility that earnings growth may not be as strong as expected. Therefore, an earnings surprise that is more positive than expected may not result in an expected price gain if the market is not supportive on that day.

Comparing Results with Previous Quarters or Periods

When interpreting a company's quarterly earnings (note that it is not mandatory to report quarterly earnings in some jurisdictions, like Hong Kong) or half-year earnings, you must compare the latest results with previous quarters or the previous half-year to see if the earnings momentum is increasing or slowing down. When analyzing such trends, take note of seasonal pattern as well.

One important fact to consider is seasonal in nature. For example, when analyzing an Asian company's earnings, take into account the slower months associated with periods that occur on festive seasons like Chinese Lunar New Year or Muslim's Hari Raya celebration (which is one of the biggest celebrations in the Muslim world, although it is technically not considered a New Year's celebration on the Muslim calendar). Also note that while the slowdown in business may be seasonal, it does not necessary fall on the same months because Chinese New Year may not fall on the same month of the western or solar calendar. It is, however, quite safe to assume that Chinese New Year will take place either in January or February of each year. And further, the Muslim calendar is shorter than the western calendar by 11 to 12 days so the Hari Raya festival may fall on a different month in different years. Therefore, a drop in revenue occurring in certain months due to seasonal attributes may not be comparable to the same period the previous years.

Generally speaking, when earnings momentum decelerates, you have to be very careful before you trade on earnings news, especially when it does not beat expectations by a wide margin.

Understanding Specific Industry Dynamics

When you interpret earnings from different industries, you should know the most important factors to look for in each industry. For example, regarding financial stocks, interest rates spreads and asset quality are the more important factors to consider when evaluating banking stocks. For insurance company shares, though, investors may place higher value on new business growth rather than pure earnings growth.

Therefore, trading earnings news on financial stocks may not be as straight forward as looking at net profit figures. In this case, you have to go through the financial statements of these companies and read the notes accompanying the financial statements.

If you are not comfortable making earnings interpretations, you may just want to skip trading, as you cannot say you are trading with an edge.

Earnings Surprises but a Cash Call

Earnings surprises should give share prices a boost most of the time. However, earnings surprises accompanied by a cash call will in most cases negate the positive price effects.

There have been instances where a company announced positive earnings that beat expectations but accompanied the announcement with a cash call in the form of rights issues of shares or, in some instances, a deferred cash call through the issuance of warrants. The price effect of the combined news is negative since investors typically do not like to put additional money into their current shareholdings. In such instances, the negative price effect triggered by the cash call more than offsets the positive price effect generated by the earnings surprise. In the end, the share price drops.

INTERPRETING RESULTS DIFFERENTLY

As we have discussed, a company in China may have shares listed in mainland China (known as A-shares) and Hong Kong (H-shares). And when the company announces its financial results, the share prices of both A-shares and H-shares may move in opposite directions.

There is usually a price differential between A-shares and H-shares. In some sectors, like financial stocks, many H-shares (especially the larger ones) tend to trade at a premium most of the time. In other sectors, like resources, A-shares usually trade at a premium over corresponding H-shares. This can be attributable to different investors' preferences.

TABLE 6.1 Yanzhou Coal Interim Results

RMB Billion	Half-Year Ending 6/30/2011	Half-Year Ending 6/30/2010	Change
Revenue	20.2	15.2	33%
Net Profit	5.2	2.7	91%
EPS (RMB)	1.05	0.55	91%

Such differences in preference can sometimes lead to prices moving in opposite directions after a company releases its financial results. As an ADR's underlying shares are of the H-shares variety, you have to be careful when interpreting the financial results.

For example, when Yanzhou Coal Mining Company Limited released its interim results for the half-year ending June 30, 2011, on August 19, 2011, the A-share and H-share prices reacted differently.

As you can see in Table 6.1, even though Yanzhou Coal reported a huge jump in earnings, Yanzhou H-shares plunged almost 9 percent on August 22, the next trading day, as the huge jump in earnings was largely attributed to foreign exchange gains. However, Yanzhou Coal A-shares reacted positively to the earnings news, rising as much as 4 percent before the plunge in H-shares caused the A-shares to close just under 1 percent higher. This illustrates that mainland Chinese investors tend to like resource companies more than their Hong Kong counterparts. As the ADRs you trade are based on the underlying H-shares, we have to interpret the result as the investors of H-shares. While it is obvious after the fact, you may incorrectly predict the share price should rise due to a surge in earnings but the share price instead plunges 9 percent. Just imagine the loss you would suffer if you acted smart and bought Yanzhou ADR on August 19.

BUYING ON RUMORS AND SELLING ON NEWS

One of the most common pitfalls in dealing with positive news or announcements is when traders buy ahead in anticipation of them and sell after they have been announced.

Because of this, you have to be very careful when dealing with positive earnings surprises when the share prices have already run ahead in anticipation of it. This usually happens when a company is on a positive earnings growth trend (or negative earnings growth or losses widening trend). When investors buy in anticipation of better than expected news, the share price reflects it so that the better-than-expected earnings, for example, are no longer the catalyst for further price gains.

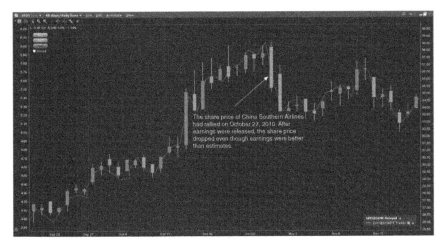

FIGURE 6.1 Price Surge of China Southern Airlines, prior to the Release of Earnings
Source: Interactive Brokers LLC.

For example, see Figure 6.1 in which the share price of China Southern Airlines Company Limited (Hong Kong Stock code: 1055; ADR Symbol: ZNH) rallied significantly, rising about 31 percent between October 1, 2010 and October 26, 2010, from HK$4.50 to HK$5.91. When the company announced third-quarter profits that came up ahead of market expectations on October 27, 2010, the "buy on rumors, sell on news" mentality came into being and the share price fell significantly after the positive earnings surprise. Traders should also note that even before October, China Southern Airlines' share price had almost doubled in price. Therefore, chasing the share on positive news was always dangerous given the substantial price gains the share had enjoyed.

BONUS ISSUE OF WARRANTS CAUSING A PRICE DROP

Some companies reward their shareholders in the form of company warrants. Company warrants that are given for free to shareholders through bonus issues are listed in the stock exchange. When shareholders get something free which can be traded in the market, you would imagine the price reaction to be positive since shareholders can sell the free warrants in the market and receive some cash. However, if the warrants issue is viewed as a deferred rights issue, the impact on the underlying share price

TABLE 6.2 Price Range of Henderson Land Development Share Price and its ADR Equivalent Price Adjusted for ADR Ratio and Exchange Rate in HK$ on the Days before and after the Bonus Issue of Warrants

Date	Actual Underlying Share Price			Equivalent ADR Price (Adjusted) ADR Price in Bracket (US$)		
	High	Low	Close	High	Low	Close
03/29/2010	58.25	55.75	56.30	55.59(7.16)	55.51(7.16)	55.51(7.15)
03/30/2010	57.65	55.75	57.10	56.68(7.30)	56.37(7.26)	56.68(7.30)
03/31/2010	57.70	54.55	54.70	55.13(7.10)	54.74(7.05)	55.13(7.10)

can be negative, as in the case of Henderson Land Development's bonus issue of warrants in March 2010.

Henderson Land Development released its earnings on March 30, 2010, for the 18-month period ending December 31, 2009. Together with the release of its financial results, Henderson Land Development announced a bonus issue of warrants on the basis of one free warrant for every five shares held. The warrants carried an exercise price of HK$58.00, which was slightly higher than the closing price of HK$57.10 on the date of the announcement. The warrant had an expiration of one year after the date of issue.

For some reason, the market interpreted the news negatively, sending Henderson Land Development's share price down about 4 percent in the next day of trading. Investors could have profited from Henderson Land Development's ADR if they interpreted the news accurately as the price of Henderson Land Development ADR had not fallen on the announcement date as illustrated in Table 6.2.

A COMPANY'S SHARE BUY BACK MAY AFFECT TRADING ON NEGATIVE NEWS

You can short a company's shares when you come across some bad news, such as an earnings disappointment. Under normal circumstances, the share price is expected to fall when earnings disappoint; traders can just go and short the share with the hope of buying back the share at a cheaper price later.

This trick may not work if the company defends the company's share price by buying back their shares in the open market. Some companies with cash reserves may buy back their shares on a regular basis. When such a company announces earnings disappointment, it may not be a good idea to short the company share because the company is defending the share price or at the very least is providing support to the share.

TABLE 6.3 Hyflux Limited Full Year Result

S$ Million	12 Months Ending 12/31/2011	12 Months Ending 12/31/2010	Change
Revenue	482.0	569.7	−15%
Net Profit	53.0	88.5	−40%
EPS (S cents)	4.3	10.5	−59%

One such example can be found in Singapore-listed Hyflux Limited. Singapore-based Hyflux Limited announced on February 22, 2012, a sharp drop in net profit for the fiscal year ending December 2011, as indicated in Table 6.3, on the back of a 15 percent drop in revenue from S$569.7 million in 2010 to S$482.0 million in 2011. The net profit of Hyflux Limited plunged 40 percent compared to 2010, from S$88.5 million a year ago to S$53 million. On a per share basis, the drop was even bigger due to an increase in the number of shares. The EPS of 4.3 cents for 2011 announced by Hyflux was close to 20 percent below the consensus estimate of 5 cents, according to *Bloomberg Businessweek.*

When such an earnings disappointment occurs, you would generally think that the share price should drop in a big way. In fact, a trader of Hyflux ADR who was short the share on the earnings disappointment on February 22, 2012, could still manage a reasonable gain of 4.6 percent when closing out the position the next day. Traders might have made more had the company not bought back its stock on February 23, 2012, following the earnings disappointment. According to an announcement made to the Singapore Stock Exchange, Hyflux bought back 1 million shares on February 23. This is significant as the cumulative number of shares repurchased prior to that day was 3.33 million. Had Hyflux not supported the price on that day, the price drop could have been much bigger.

To be fair to the company, Hyflux was not just buying back its shares to support the price after an earnings disappointment. In fact, the company regularly repurchases its shares from the open market, as it had a cash

TABLE 6.4 Hyflux Actual Underlying Share Price and Equivalent ADR Price

Date	Actual Underlying Share Price			Equivalent ADR Price (adjusted) ADR Price in Bracket (US$)		
	High	Low	Close	High	Low	Close
02/21/2012	1.55	1.47	1.53	1.52(24.26)	1.50(23.95)	1.50(24.05)
02/22/2012	1.58	1.50	1.58	1.55(24.68)	1.55(24.68)	1.55(24.68)
02/23/2012	1.53	1.43	1.47	1.48(23.55)	1.48(23.55)	1.48(23.55)

position of some S$662 million as at the end of 2011, about half of its market capitalization. Buying back its own shares may be a good use of the company's large cash holdings. The company had actually stepped up the pace of share repurchase after the earnings disappointment. See Table 6.4.

WHEN A PIECE OF NEWS GETS UPSTAGED BY A MORE IMPACTFUL PIECE OF NEWS

Sometimes you discover some price-sensitive news that you think might move the market the next day. While that particular piece of news may impact the share price somewhat, if you go ahead and buy or short the ADR, there may be another piece of news that occurs the next day that negates the price direction of the underlying share.

For example, China raised the retail prices of gasoline and diesel by 6 to 7 percent on March 20, 2012, the biggest increase in 33 months. Although the price increase was widely expected, the quantum of increase of RMB 600/mt was higher than the market expectation of RMB 500/mt. This piece of news was already known in the evening in Asia on March 19. Traders would naturally think that such news would benefit refiners like Sinopec, and hence Sinopec ADR could be bought on March 19 at a slight premium to the equivalent Hong Kong closing price. As this piece of news was carried by major Western news media very early, there was already some slight upward impact on the Sinopec ADR price. Nevertheless, traders may long Sinopec ADR with the expectation that the underlying share could surge the next day in Hong Kong.

However, the Sinopec share price actually fell 3 percent on March 20 after another piece of news about the company's rumored bond issuance broke along with a less-than-upbeat report by brokers on the oil price hike impact for Sinopec's refining profitability. Traders who bought Sinopec ADR ahead on March 19 would thus suffer losses on this particular trade.

Another incident occurred when Li Ka-Shing's Cheung Kong Holdings reported a 72 percent jump in net profit for the year ending 2011, to HK$46.06 billion on March 29, 2012. The earnings achieved were significantly higher than analysts' estimates of HK$39 billion to HK$43 billion. However, the share price was down on the next trading day, as the whole property sector in Hong Kong was negatively affected by the arrest of joint-chairmen from one of the largest developers in the world, Sun Hung Kai Properties, in the highest profile corruption case on record in Hong Kong.

The risk of encountering more impactful news that is price sensitive would be difficult to avoid if it takes place in the next trading days after the initial price-moving news which traders took advantage of the previous day. Therefore, trading on such news is not a sure bet, as you are still exposed to what happens the next trading day in the underlying share's home market.

SUMMARY

Having access to price-sensitive information ahead of most other players gives you a definite trading advantage. This is, however, not a 100 percent sure thing. There are many factors that can reduce and sometimes eliminate the impact of such sensitive news on the share price direction.

Some of these price mitigation factors have been discussed in this chapter but there are other things at play not covered here. It is therefore very important for traders to maintain good money management principles even when dealing with what seem like such clear advantages.

We have completed the theoretical part for using after-hours market news from Asia to trade U.S. ADRs.

To add to the proof, the next few chapters look at some case studies from the past where traders traded ADRs profitably. It also separates the types of news that you can use into different chapters and gives you some examples of each type of news.

PART II

ADR Case Studies

CHAPTER 7

Case Study 1: An Earnings Surprise

When a listed company announces financial results that beat market expectations, it is very likely the share price will move up if it has not already run ahead of the earnings announcements. Even if the share price has run up, it still has some room to go if the result is way ahead of estimates or there are some significant developments in the company that warrant further upward momentum.

For example, if a division within a conglomerate that has been making losses throughout the years suddenly returns to black and signals further positive results, it is likely that many investors who had not factored in such a turnaround would be interested in buying into it. The share price would also get further boosts if there are short sellers expecting such losses to continue and need to close their short positions by buying back the shares.

In this chapter, we offer some case studies where traders can take advantage of earnings surprises for underlying companies listed in Asia after hours and take up positions in their corresponding ADRs. When the underlying share price does indeed go up the next day, traders can then sell the ADRs the following day and make relatively safe profits out of such information.

LENOVO GROUP LIMITED

On November 2, 2011, Lenovo Group Limited, China's largest computing hardware manufacturer, announced its 2011 half-year results after Asian trading hours.

TABLE 7.1 Lenovo Group Interim Results

US$ Million	3 Months Ending 9/30/2011	3 Months Ending 9/30/2010	Change
Revenue	7,786.4	5,760.0	35%
Net Profit	143.9	76.6	88%
EPS (U.S. Cents)	1.41	0.81	74%
Diluted EPS (U.S. Cents)	1.38	0.76	82%

Table 7.1 shows that Lenovo achieved a 35 percent rise in revenue, to US$7.8 billion, in the quarter ending September 30, 2011, as compared to US$5.8 billion recorded for the corresponding period in 2010. Net profit came in at US$143.9 million, compared to US$76.6 million achieved in the quarter ending September 30, 2010.

According to a Dow Jones Newswire poll at that time, analysts had been expecting Lenovo's quarterly revenue to be around US$7.2 billion. The average analysts' forecast for Lenovo's net profit was only US$117.8 million.

Lenovo's net profit, at US$143.9 million, was 22 percent ahead of analysts' forecast then. This set of results was released to the Hong Kong Stock Exchange after market closing. What could we have done with the results?

Lenovo has a sponsored ADR (Stock Symbol: LNVGY) listed on OTC market in the United States. The exchange ratio for the ADR was 1 for 20 underlying shares and the ADR was trading between US$14.31 to US$14.53 on November 2 in the United States, after the earnings news was understood by people.

Based on the exchange rate of that day of HK$7.7636/US$, Lenovo ADR was trading at the equivalent price of HK$5.55 to HK$5.64. The closing price of Lenovo's underlying share in Hong Kong on November 2, 2011, was HK$5.60.

As Lenovo's actual results were more than 20 percent higher than analysts' expectations, it was highly likely that Lenovo's share price would surge when it resumed trading the next day. With such information, you can be reasonably sure that Lenovo's share price would go up on November 3, so by buying into Lenovo's ADR at the closing price of US$14.41 on November 2 you can profit from such earnings news.

The surge in share price indeed took place and Lenovo's underlying share in Hong Kong rose as much as 8 percent on November 3 before closing still close to 4 percent up at HK$5.78, as indicated in Table 7.2.

For the traders who bought Lenovo's ADR on November 2 at US$14.41, they would have made a gain of 5 percent, assuming they sold at the closing price of US$15.14 the next day.

	Actual Underlying Share Price			Equivalent ADR Price (Adjusted) ADR Price in Brackets (US$)		
TABLE 7.2 Price Range of Lenovo Share Price and its ADR Equivalent Price Adjusted for ADR Ratio and Exchange Rate in HK$ on Days before and after the Earnings Surprise						
Date	**High**	**Low**	**Close**	**High**	**Low**	**Close**
11/01/2011	5.38	5.22	5.34	5.26(13.55)	5.18(13.35)	5.18(13.35)
11/02/2011	5.63	5.25	5.60	5.64(14.53)	5.55(14.31)	5.59(14.41)
11/03/2011	6.04	5.61	5.78	5.88(15.15)	5.74(14.79)	5.88(15.14)

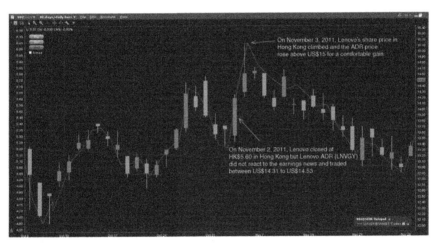

FIGURE 7.1   Lenovo Price Chart
Source: Interactive Brokers LLC.

Figure 7.1 illustrates the price reaction of LNVGY and its underlying share Lenovo (stock code: 992) in the Hong Kong Stock Exchange on the days leading up to and after the earnings surprise on November 2, 2011.

GUANGSHEN RAILWAY COMPANY LIMITED

After the close of Asian trading hours on April 14, 2011, Guangshen Railway Company released its first quarter results for the period ended March 31, 2011. The company reported revenue of RMB3.4 billion, a 13 percent rise compared to RMB3.0 billion the same period in 2010 as indicated in Table 7.3.

TABLE 7.3 Guangshen Railway 2011Q1 Results

RMB Million	3 Months Ending 3/31/2011	3 Months Ending 3/31/2010	Change
Revenue	3,411.1	3,023.6	13%
Net Profit	418.8	282.9	48%
EPS (RMB Cents)	5.9	4.0	48%

TABLE 7.4 Price Range of Guangshen Railway Share Price and its ADR Equivalent Price Adjusted for ADR Ratio and Exchange Rate in HK$ on the Days before and after the Earnings Surprise

Date	Actual Underlying Share Price			Equivalent ADR Price (Adjusted) ADR Price in Brackets (US$)		
	High	Low	Close	High	Low	Close
04/13/2011	3.04	2.97	3.03	3.03(19.49)	2.98(19.18)	3.00(19.26)
04/14/2011	3.03	3.00	3.01	3.03(19.46)	2.97(19.12)	3.02(19.45)
04/15/2011	3.13	3.06	3.13	3.12(20.10)	3.06(19.67)	3.11(20.00)

The net profit of Guangshen Railway for the period surged 48 percent from RMB 282.9 billion to RMB418.8 billion. This was higher than expected by just under 10 percent. What is more significant, though, is the momentum of earnings growth which accelerated to 48 percent from −10 percent in the fourth quarter of 2010 and 32 percent in the third quarter 2010.

Traders who were alerted to the Guangshen Railway results released on April 14, 2011, could buy Guangshen Railway ADR (GSH) at more or less the same price listed earlier in the day in Hong Kong, where the underlying share was listed between US$19.12 to US$19.46—equivalent to HK$2.97 to HK$3.03—which is within the price range traded in Hong Kong earlier in the day as indicated on Table 7.4. Guangshen ADR is a sponsored ADR that is listed on the New York Stock Exchange with an ADR exchange ratio of 1 for 50 underlying shares.

Assuming you bought Guangshen Railway ADR at the closing price of US$19.45 on April 14, 2011, you would be able to make a quick profit the next day when the Hong Kong underlying share price rose about 4 percent. If Guangshen ADR closed at US$20.00 on April 15, 2011, and you would be able to make close to 3 percent.

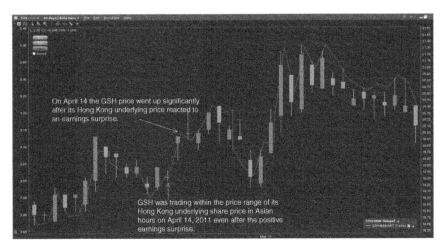

FIGURE 7.2 Guangshen Railway Price Chart
Source: Interactive Brokers LLC.

Figure 7.2 illustrates the price reaction of GSH and its underlying share Guangshen Railway (stock code: 525) in the Hong Kong Stock Exchange on the days leading up to and after the earnings surprise on April 14, 2011.

If you are not satisfied with a 3 percent overnight gain, you could trade the options of Guangshen ADR. The stock options of Guangshen Railway ADR are available for traders even though there is not much interest in relatively quiet securities like Guangshen Railway.

Nevertheless, the May 2011 in-the-money call option for Guangshen Railway, with a strike price of US$17.50, could have been bought at a premium of about US$1.95 based on the theoretical price calculated from market-maker quotes. If you chose an in-the-money call option because the earnings did not beat expectations by a lot, choosing the next-month option then prevents you from suffering rapid time decay, as the expiration date for April 2011 fell on the next day.

If you had done this, the price of the mentioned call option would have risen to about US$2.45 based on the theoretical price calculated on that day. This would give you an overnight gain of 25 percent.

However, you have to be careful when dealing with such thinly traded stock options because the bid-ask spread is rather wide and you have to be patient in order for your trades to be filled. Traders should also be reminded that options trading have substantial risks. Unless you are very familiar and comfortable with options trading, buying the underlying share on margin or trading it through a CFD would be a relatively easier process, as this particular stock option was thinly traded.

TABLE 7.5 Yanzhou Coal 2010Q3 Results

RMB Million	3 Months Ending 9/30/2010	3 Months Ending 9/30/2009	Change
Revenue	9,349.4	5,722.5	64%
Net Profit	3,680.7	1,124.2	227%
EPS (RMB)	0.75	0.23	226%

TABLE 7.6 Price Range of Yanzhou Coal Share Price and its ADR Equivalent Price Adjusted for ADR Ratio and Exchange Rate in HK$ on Days before and after the Earnings Surprise

Date	Actual Underlying Share Price			Equivalent ADR Price (Adjusted) ADR Price in Brackets (US$)		
	High	Low	Close	High	Low	Close
10/21/2010	21.95	21.40	21.80	21.95(28.27)	21.33(27.48)	21.65(27.89)
10/22/2010	22.00	21.20	21.75	22.07(28.44)	21.45(27.64)	21.97(28.31)
10/25/2010	24.20	22.15	24.10	24.23(31.23)	23.70(30.55)	23.99(30.93)

YANZHOU COAL MINING COMPANY

Yanzhou Coal Mining Company Limited released its report for the third quarter of 2010 shortly after the Hong Kong market closed on October 22, 2010. See Table 7.5.

Yanzhou Coal reported a 64 percent jump in revenue compared to the same period in the third quarter of 2009 while net profit surged 227 percent from RMB1.1 billion to RMB3.7 billion. The results were above the expectations of analysts' estimates. More importantly, the company indicated in their quarterly report that the full year profit for 2010 would double that of 2009, implying fourth quarter profits would be strong as well.

One important factor that would possibly trigger the share price to surge the next day was that the third quarter profit was higher than the combined first two quarters' profit, suggesting earnings were accelerating.

After the third-quarter report was released after Asian trading hours on October 22, the NYSE-listed ADR of Yanzhou Coal (YZC) did not seem to react to the earnings surprise, as indicated in Table 7.6. Adjusting for the exchange rate and an ADR ratio of 10, Yanzhou Coal ADR could still be bought within the price range traded earlier that day in Hong Kong. This allowed smart traders who were alerted to Yanzhou Coal's earnings news to buy the ADR.

On the next trading day in Hong Kong—the Monday after Yanzhou Coal's earnings report was digested—the share price surged more than 10 percent to close at HK$24.10 on October 25. This was indeed a jackpot for those who bought the ADR on October 22.

Yanzhou Coal ADR, as expected, rose just under 10 percent on October 25 to close at US$30.93. This gave traders who bought the ADR with the knowledge of the earnings report a spectacular overnight return. See Table 7.6.

As with the previous case of Guangshen Railway ADR, traders could have made much more profit with the call options of Yanzhou Coal.

Unlike Guangshen Railway options, which attracted very little buying and selling, Yanzhou Coal options were better supported. Assuming you managed to buy the at-the-money (strike price of US$28) November call option of YZC on October 22 at the closing ask price of US$1.45, you would be able to sell the option the next trading day (October 25) at a price of at least US$3.10 (based on the closing bid price). This would give you a gain of 114 percent had you acted on the earnings surprise using leverage.

Had you been a little more aggressive and opted to buy the out-of-the-money call option with a strike price of US$30 on October 22, you would have been able to get the call option at about US$0.50 and sold the option the next trading day at US$1.75. This position would have given you a return of 250 percent.

Figure 7.3 indicates that a trader who acted on October 22 and bought Yanzhou Coal ADR (YZC) would make a substantial return on the next trading day.

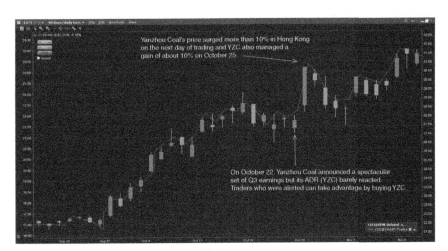

FIGURE 7.3 Yanzhou Coal Price Chart
Source: Interactive Brokers LLC.

CHINA UNICOM (HONG KONG) LIMITED

China Unicom, the second largest telecommunications company in China, reported a stunning set of results after the market closed in Asia on August 24, 2011.

While the market expected a sharp drop in profit for China Unicom, with the consensus estimates at RMB1.2 billion to RMB1.3 billion, the company reported much higher net profit—RMB2.6 billion—as indicated in Table 7.7.

What made the results much more bullish was the chairman's statement in the result note that he expected the outlook for the second half to show significant improvement in profitability. This is a situation when the financial results and forward guidance of the company caught the investment community by surprise.

Because such a bullish statement came from a company when not very much was expected of them, we all knew that the share price would run riot the next day.

Since China Unicom is a relatively well-known company, the results did not go unnoticed in the United States and its ADR traded higher compared to its Hong Kong underlying price on August 24, 2011, as indicated in Table 7.8. In fact, the ADR price ended close to 8 percent higher than the underlying price in Hong Kong. It should also be noted that the broader U.S. stock market also rose more than 1 percent on August 24.

TABLE 7.7   China Unicom 2011 Interim Results

RMB Million	6 Months Ending 6/30/2011	6 Months Ending 6/30/2010	Change
Revenue	101,400	82,640	22%
Net Profit	2,652	2,922	−6%
EPS (RMB)	0.11	0.12	−9%

TABLE 7.8   Price Range of China Unicom Share Price and its ADR Equivalent Price Adjusted for ADR Ratio and Exchange Rate in HK$ on the Days before and after the Earnings Surprise

Date	Actual Underlying Share Price			Equivalent ADR Price (Adjusted) ADR Price in Brackets (US$)		
	High	Low	Close	High	Low	Close
08/23/2011	13.70	13.22	13.66	14.02(17.98)	13.53(17.35)	13.99(17.95)
08/24/2011	13.96	13.48	13.74	15.04(19.30)	14.09(18.08)	14.83(19.03)
08/25/2011	15.76	14.78	15.38	15.78(20.24)	15.43(19.79)	15.47(19.84)

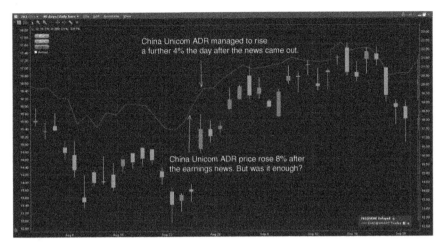

FIGURE 7.4   Price Chart of China Unicom
Source: Interactive Brokers LLC.

As this particular piece of news was way ahead of estimates and the bullish statement by the company was totally unexpected, you know that the ADR price might still have a few more percentage to run the next day after Hong Kong reacted to the news.

Figure 7.4 indicates China Unicom surged further on August 25, the day after the news was released, even though it had risen 8 percent on August 24.

This indicates that opportunities in bigger ADR names are still possible but you have to know the companies very well. It is essential to build a watch list of companies to monitor closely and make sure you have sufficient knowledge on the companies and how the investment community in Asia is viewing the company at any time.

While it may not be a no-brainer, you can still churn out profitable trades on the bigger-name ADRs that some U.S. investors may be familiar with. However, it is still much easier to make money on lesser-known names, where the market makers are just there to provide liquidity based on the Asian trading range of the underlying share.

SUMMARY

We looked at case studies of earnings surprises in this chapter, using a number of Chinese companies as examples about how profits can be made comfortably using information available after the Asian market closes.

Next up, earnings shocks! Chapter 8 offers examples of companies failing to meet earnings expectations and how traders can profit from such misfortunes.

Case Study 2: Earnings Disappointments

After dealing with earnings surprises in the previous chapter, let's turn our attention to an earnings disappointment case, where a company reports profit coming in below the analysts' forecast. In this situation, traders can short the corresponding ADR or buy the related put options to enjoy the information advantage gained before the underlying share has a chance to react when trading resumes in Asia the next day.

LI & FUNG LIMITED

Li & Fung announced, after the Asia market closed on March 24, 2011, that its revenue for the financial year ending 2010 recorded a gain of 19 percent to HK$124.1 billion from HK$104.5 billion in 2009, as illustrated in Table 8.1. The company's net profit rose 27 percent to HK$4.3 billion from HK$3.4 billion a year ago. Li & Fung's earnings per share for 2010 increased 23 percent to 111.9 cents. This is significantly below the consensus analysts' estimate of approximately 130.0 cents according to Bloomberg's survey then.

TABLE 8.1 Li & Fung Final Results

HK$ Million	12 Months Ending 12/31/2010	12 Months Ending 12/31/2009	Change
Revenue	124,115	104,479	19%
Core Operating Profit	5,656	3,990	42%
Net Profit	4,278	3,369	27%
EPS (HK Cents)	111.9	91.0	23%

When you come across such a piece of information, you should take a look at the underlying ADR to see if there is any opportunity to make some money. Li & Fung does not have a sponsored ADR. Its unsponsored ADR (LFUGY) has a few depository banks.

On March 24, the day when the results were released, Li & Fung ADR was traded between US$5.40 and US$5.56. This is equivalent to HK$21.04 to HK$21.67 after adjusted to the ADR ratio of 2 for 1 as indicated in Table 8.2. The price illustrated in Table 8.2 was retroactively adjusted for a stock split undertaken by Li & Fung in April 2011.

With the disappointment in earnings, we foresee the price of Li & Fung will fall significantly on March 25 in Hong Kong after a negative investors' reaction.

TABLE 8.2   Price Range of Li & Fung Share Price and its ADR Equivalent Price Adjusted for ADR Ratio and Exchange Rate in HK$ on the Days before and after an Earnings Disappointment

Date	Actual Underlying Share Price			Equivalent ADR Price (Adjusted) ADR Price in Brackets (US$)		
	High	Low	Close	High	Low	Close
03/23/2011	21.58	21.20	21.55	21.71(5.57)	21.32(5.47)	21.59(5.54)
03/24/2011	22.12	21.45	21.48	21.67(5.56)	21.04(5.40)	21.36(5.48)
03/25/2011	20.25	19.48	19.52	21.55(5.53)	19.49(5.00)	19.52(5.01)

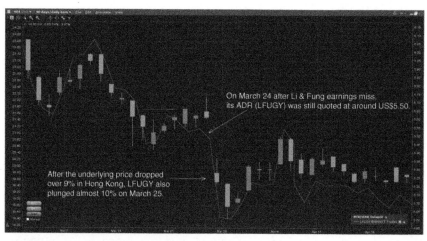

On March 24 after Li & Fung earnings miss, its ADR (LFUGY) was still quoted at around US$5.50.

After the underlying price dropped over 9% in Hong Kong, LFUGY also plunged almost 10% on March 25.

FIGURE 8.1   Li & Fung Price Chart

Source: Interactive Brokers LLC.

Li & Fung's underlying share, as expected, fell more than 9 percent on March 25 and those traders who short sold Li & Fung ADR managed to pocket a significant return of about 10 percent trading on the earnings disappointment as illustrated in Figure 8.1, showing the price reaction of Li & Fung ADR and its underlying share in the Hong Kong Stock Exchange on the days leading up to and after the earnings disappointment on March 24, 2011.

YANZHOU COAL MINING COMPANY

Traders should keep Yanzhou Coal Mining Company on their watch list as it is not big enough to attract mainstream news coverage in the west but its ADR is large enough to have good liquidity in both the ADR and its call and put options. Yanzhou Coal is featured as a case study of a company announcing earnings that beat estimates. It is also a case where the company did not meet earnings expectations and provided an opportunity for traders to short its shares. This incident actually took place earlier in October 2009. On October 27, 2009, Yanzhou Coal released its third-quarter results after the market closed in Asia.

Yanzhou Coal reported a 25 percent drop in revenue compared to the same period in the third quarter of 2008, while net profit sank 61 percent, from RMB2.9 billion to RMB1.1 billion. The results announced were a disappointment to the market. This led to possible play on the down side. See Table 8.3.

Even though you could easily short Yanzhou Coal ADR on the earnings disappointment, it would have been a better strategy to buy a put option on Yanzhou Coal. As illustrated in Table 8.4, Yanzhou Coal ADR was trading between US$15.84 and US$16.91 on October 27, closing on the lower end of the price range at US$16.03. If you were to be conservative and buy into an in-the-money put option with a strike price of US$17.50 expiring in November 2009, the premium you would pay would be US$1.90.

TABLE 8.3 Yanzhou Coal 2009Q3 Results

RMB Million	3 Months Ending 9/30/2009	3 Months Ending 9/30/2008	Change
Revenue	5,722.5	7,678.3	−25%
Net Profit	1,124.2	2,903.8	−61%
EPS (RMB)	0.23	0.59	−61%

TABLE 8.4	Price Range of Yanzhou Coal Share Price and its ADR Equivalent Price Adjusted for ADR Ratio and Exchange Rate in HK$ on the Days before and after an Earnings Disappointment

	Actual Underlying Share Price			Equivalent ADR Price (Adjusted) ADR Price in Brackets (US$)		
Date	High	Low	Close	High	Low	Close
10/26/2009	Public	Holiday		16.88(13.08)	16.22(12.57)	16.45(12.75)
10/27/2009	12.8	12.3	12.58	16.91(13.10)	15.84(12.28)	16.03(12.42)
10/28/2009	12.62	12.32	12.34	15.97(12.38)	15.11(11.71)	15.16(11.75)

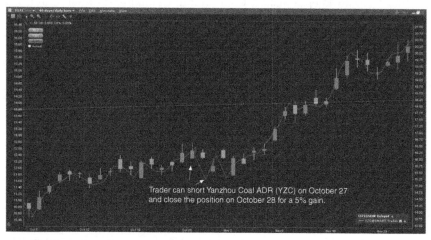

FIGURE 8.2   Yanzhou Coal Price Chart
Source: Interactive Brokers LLC.

Yanzhou Coal's underlying share then dropped around 2 percent when the market resumed on October 28. This in turn led to Yanzhou Coal ADR sinking more than 5.4 percent the next day (which was a weak day in the U.S. market).

While you could have made slightly more than 5 percent shorting Yanzhou Coal ADR on October 27, 2009, and closing it the next day, the gain in the Yanzhou Coal put option was much bigger. The in-the-money put option that you could have bought on October 27 for US$1.90 rose more than 21 percent to US$2.30. Buying a put option to trade on such bad news is a better option than shorting the stock since it need not involve putting up a margin to short the stocks. You can also not worry about a potential margin call if your trade significantly goes the wrong way. Figure 8.2 illustrates the price reaction of Yanzhou Coal ADR and its underlying share in the Hong Kong Stock Exchange on the days leading up to and after the earnings disappointment on October 27, 2009.

CHINA SHENHUA ENERGY COMPANY LIMITED

China Shenhua posted earnings that were short of market expectation on March 12, 2012. For the financial year ending 2009, China Shenhua reported a revenue growth of 13 percent to RMB121.3 billion from RMB107.1 billion in 2008 as indicated in Table 8.5. Even though the company's net profit grew 19 percent from RMB26.6 billion to RMB31.7 billion, most analysts had expected more.

China Shenhua's ADR is an unsponsored one listed on the Pink OTC Market. Due to its relatively low profile, traders can often take advantage of this unsponsored ADR. After the earnings report was released on Friday, March 12, the ADR of China Shenhua did not decline, as shown in Table 8.6. This provided an opportunity to short the ADR.

When China Shenhua's underlying share resumed trading in Hong Kong the next trading day, Monday, March 15, the share dropped almost 4 percent. Traders who managed to short China Shenhua's ADR could then close the position on Monday with a gain of about 3 percent.

TABLE 8.5 China Shenhua 2009 Financial Year Results

RMB Million	12 Months Ending 12/31/2009	12 Months Ending 12/31/2008	Change
Revenue	121,312	107,133	13%
Net Profit	31,706	26,641	19%
EPS (RMB)	1.594	1.339	19%

TABLE 8.6 Price Range of China Shenhua Share Price and its ADR Equivalent Price Adjusted for ADR Ratio and Exchange Rate in HK$ on the Days before and after an Earnings Surprise

	Actual Underlying Share Price			Equivalent ADR Price (Adjusted) ADR Price in Brackets (US$)		
Date	High	Low	Close	High	Low	Close
03/11/2010	35.40	34.60	34.90	35.38(45.60)	35.30(45.50)	35.30(45.50)
03/12/2010	35.20	34.55	34.70	38.26(49.33)	34.91(45.00)	34.91(45.00)
03/15/2010	34.35	33.20	33.35	33.94(43.75)	33.25(42.85)	33.94(43.75)

FIGURE 8.3   China Shenhua Price Chart

Source: Interactive Brokers LLC.

Figure 8.3 illustrates the price reaction of China Shenhua's ADR and its underlying share in the Hong Kong Stock Exchange on the days leading up to and after the earnings disappointment on March 12, 2010.

HUANENG POWER INTERNATIONAL INC.

Huaneng Power International is another company that traders should keep on their watch list. While the company is not famous enough to attract a large following for its ADR, it is listed on the New York Stock Exchange and has listed equity options. Another unusual attribute of this company is that it usually releases its earnings late in the evening in Asia. This means there is very little coverage of the earnings news no matter how significant it is because most Asian-based reporters are already off for the day.

Since 2010, all interim and final results of Huaneng Power International have been released to the stock exchange after 9:00 p.m. in Hong Kong as indicated in Table 8.7. This gives traders who follow Huaneng Power International closely opportunities to make money from news released after Asian trading hours.

On March 20, 2012, Huaneng Power International released its final results for the financial year 2011, late in the evening. The company managed to increase its revenue by 28 percent, from RMB104.3 billion to RMB 133.4 billion, as shown in Table 8.8. However, net profit achieved by Huaneng Power International plunged 65 percent to RMB1.18 billion from

TABLE 8.7	The Timing of the Release of Huaneng Power International's Interim and Final Results

Release Time	Item
03/20/2012—22:57	Announcements and Notices—[Final Results/Dividend or Distribution]
08/09/2011—21:44	Announcements and Notices—[Interim Results/Price-Sensitive Information]
03/29/2011—22:54	Announcements and Notices—[Final Results/Dividend or Distribution]
08/10/2010—22:24	Announcements and Notices—[Interim Results/Price-Sensitive Information]
03/23/2010—22:42	Announcements and Notices—[Final Results/Dividend or Distribution]

Source: HKEx.

TABLE 8.8   Huaneng Power International Final Results

RMB Million	12 Months Ending 12/31/2011	12 Months Ending 12/31/2010	Change
Revenue	133,420	104,318	28%
Net Profit	1,181	3,348	−65%
EPS (RMB)	0.08	0.28	−71%

TABLE 8.9   Brokers' Profit Estimates for Huaneng Power International

Financial Year	Profit/(Loss) (M)(RMB (MIL))	EPS/(Loss) (RMB (cts))	DPS (cts)(RMB (cts))	Highest (M) (RMB (MIL))	Lowest (M) (RMB (MIL))
12/2011	1,605.00	11.5	6	1,773.00	1,437.00
12/2012	6,069.50	43	25	6,956.00	5,183.00
12/2013	6,412.00	46	23	6,412.00	6,412.00

Source: ET Net. Limited—www.etnet.com.hk

RMB3.35 billion in 2010. This is well below the consensus net profit estimate of RMB1.6 billion according to data compiled by ET Net as indicated in Table 8.9.

Since the actual earnings are close to 30 percent below brokers' estimates, you can be reasonably sure that Huaneng Power International's price will fall steeply the next day. As the ADR had not dropped on March 20,

TABLE 8.10 Price Range of Huaneng Power International Share Price and its ADR Equivalent Price Adjusted for ADR Ratio and Exchange Rate in HK$ on the Days before and after an Earnings Shock

Date	Actual Underlying Share Price			Equivalent ADR Price (Adjusted) ADR Price in Brackets (US$)		
	High	Low	Close	High	Low	Close
03/19/2012	4.73	4.61	4.62	4.69(24.15)	4.62(23.82)	4.64(23.89)
03/20/2012	4.81	4.59	4.66	4.69(24.17)	4.63(23.88)	4.68(24.09)
03/21/2012	4.61	4.20	4.31	4.48(23.07)	4.30(22.15)	4.34(22.38)

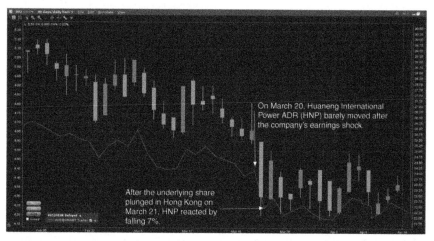

FIGURE 8.4 Price Chart of Huaneng Power International (HNP)
Source: Interactive Brokers LLC.

you could seize the opportunity by shorting Huaneng Power International's ADR. The stock fell 7.5 percent in Hong Kong on March 21 and you would have pocketed a profit of 7 percent by closing the short ADR position.

However, you can actually make more money if you choose to buy Huaneng International Power's ADR put option. On March 20, you could have bought the ADR April 2012 in-the-money put option with a strike price of US$25.00 for a premium of US$1.40 based on the closing ask price of the option. Then, when the stock falls the next day, the put option price will surge to more than US$2.40 based on the bid price at the close. Please note however that this option was not traded on that day and we could probably have sold it at closer to US$3.00 for a 100 percent gain based on the midpoint of the bid-ask spread. Figure 8.4 indicates that HNP plunged on March 21, 2012, which is the next day after the earnings shock.

SUMMARY

You can make money trading ADRs when companies beat or miss earnings expectations. Chapters 7 and 8 offer case studies on how to trade profitably when companies come up with earnings surprises and shocks.

Besides earnings news, what other news can you use to trade ADRs profitably? The next chapter looks at government policy changes that can have an impact on share price and offers some real-life examples.

CHAPTER 9

Case Study 3: Government Policy Changes

The Chinese government does not have control over the price of crude oil because it is determined by international supply and demand. However, it does exercise control over domestic refined oil products such as gasoline and diesels through the National Development and Reform Commission (NDRC).

The NDRC typically announces oil price adjustments in the evening for new prices that go into effect at midnight. As the stock market in Asia is already closed for trading at that time, there is some opportunity for traders to trade on the ADRs of Chinese energy companies listed in the United States, especially when the price adjustment announcements are unexpected.

SINOPEC—MARCH 24, 2009

China's NDRC announced on the evening of March 24, 2009, that it would raise the benchmark retail prices of gasoline and diesel by 290 yuan per ton and 180 yuan per ton respectively. This was the first time in four months that the government raised the price of oil products and the second adjustment in 2009 after a price cut in January of that same year. China had previously adjusted oil prices more infrequently and this latest adjustment was a little unexpected.

An unexpected price increase in domestic refined oil products would benefit companies with significant refining businesses such as Sinopec. Even though PetroChina also has refining operations, the impact would be higher on Sinopec, as PetroChina has significant exploration and oil production operations that are not affected by domestic refined product price changes.

This price adjustment news came in on the evening of March 24, after the stock market closed in Asia. However, the ADR of Sinopec had not reacted to the positive news on March 24 in New York, as illustrated in Table 9.1.

Traders who were alerted to the domestic oil price adjustment on March 24 could benefit from the expected positive price impact by buying Sinopec's ADR which closed at US$57.21 or the equivalent of HK$4.43. This was about the same price Sinopec closed at in Hong Kong earlier in the day.

When the market resumed trading the next day, Sinopec shares managed to record a gain of 5.4 percent despite the fact that the broader market suffered a sharp drop with the Hang Seng Index falling 2 percent on March 25. Sinopec ADR rose over 6 percent later that day to US$60.80 and traders who bought Sinopec ADR the day before realized their profit.

Traders who were more aggressive could have used Sinopec ADR call options to enhance their trading gain with a piece of news like this. You could choose the slightly out-of-money April 2009 call option with a strike price of US$60.00 which was calling for US$2.50 at the close of March 24 (although the last traded price was higher than US$3.00), as illustrated in Table 9.2.

TABLE 9.1 Price Range of Sinopec (0386) Share Price and its ADR Equivalent Price Adjusted for ADR Ratio and Exchange Rate in HK$ on the Days before and after the Government Adjusts Oil Prices

	Actual Underlying Share Price			Equivalent ADR Price (Adjusted) ADR Price in Brackets (US$)		
Date	High	Low	Close	High	Low	Close
03/23/2009	4.33	4.15	4.32	4.50(58.10)	4.28(55.21)	4.50(58.10)
03/24/2009	4.47	4.35	4.40	4.59(59.19)	4.35(56.12)	4.43(57.21)
03/25/2009	4.85	4.55	4.64	4.78(61.69)	4.59(59.20)	4.71(60.80)

TABLE 9.2 April 2009 Call Options Prices of Sinopec on March 24, 2009

Strike	Bid	Ask	Last
50	8.10	8.90	8.80
55	4.60	5.00	5.40
60	2.25	2.50	3.00
65	0.85	1.00	0.90

TABLE 9.3 April 2009 Call Options Prices of Sinopec on March 25, 2009

Strike	Bid	Ask	Last
50	10.60	11.70	10.97
55	6.80	7.40	6.70
60	3.80	4.10	4.00
65	1.50	1.70	1.50

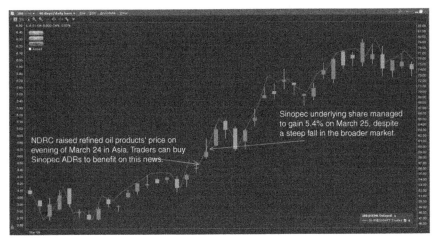

FIGURE 9.1 Price Chart of Sinopec and its ADR

Source: Interactive Brokers LLC.

When Sinopec's price surged the next day, buyers of the US$60 strike price Sinopec call then closed the position at about US$4.00 for a gain of 60 percent, as shown in Table 9.3.

Figure 9.1 indicates Sinopec's share surged upon the refined oil products price adjustment by the NDRC.

SINOPEC—JULY 28, 2009

On the evening of July 28, 2009, China's National Development and Reform Commission announced that it would cut gasoline and diesel prices by about 3 percent starting at midnight on July 29, 2009.

If an increase in refinery product prices benefits Sinopec, a cut in price is not good news for Sinopec. Traders could therefore trade on the downward price adjustment news by short selling Sinopec's ADR or buying ADR put options.

Sinopec's ADR was trading at US$90.25 on July 28, 2009, down 2 percent as compared to the equivalent underlying share price in Hong Kong, as indicated in Table 9.4. This could be a tough decision for traders to call because the stock has already fallen a bit and the price reaction in Hong Kong the next day might not be enough to justify a punt on the trade.

Given that Sinopec's ADR already dropped a bit, you may not want to risk your share margin account in shorting Sinopec's ADR. Fortunately, Sinopec put options are available and it allows you to trade a speculative view on the ADR without risking too much of your capital.

The environment prevailing then should lead you to buy an at-the-money put with a strike price of US$90.00 expiring August 2009. This put option was selling at a price of US$3.99 on July 28, 2009. If you had bought it and waited one day after the underlying share in Hong Kong suffered a 5 percent drop, you would have made a profit of more than 50 percent by selling the put option at US$6.10 on July 29, 2009. (See Tables 9.5 and 9.6.)

Figure 9.2 indicates Sinopec's share price fell upon the refined oil products price adjustment by the NDRC.

Please bear in mind that in order to profit from China's refined oil products' price adjustments, the price adjustments must not be anticipated as the share price may have already reacted in anticipation of the adjustment.

TABLE 9.4 Price Range of Sinopec (0386) Share Price and its ADR Equivalent Price Adjusted for ADR Ratio and Exchange Rate in HK$ on the Days before and after the Government Adjusts Oil Prices

	Actual Underlying Share Price			Equivalent ADR Price (Adjusted) ADR Price in Brackets (US$)		
Date	High	Low	Close	High	Low	Close
07/27/2009	7.20	7.03	7.09	7.18(92.68)	7.04(90.83)	7.11(91.77)
07/28/2009	7.17	7.01	7.14	7.01(90.51)	6.88(88.76)	6.99(90.25)
07/29/2009	7.00	6.60	6.78	6.77(87.30)	6.61(85.33)	6.68(86.25)

TABLE 9.5 August 2009 Call Options Prices of Sinopec on July 28, 2009

Strike	Bid	Ask	Last
80	0.75	0.90	0.89
85	1.85	2.05	2.40
90	3.80	4.10	3.99
95	6.70	7.10	7.40

TABLE 9.6 August 2009 Call Options Prices of Sinopec on July 29, 2009

Strike	Bid	Ask	Last
80	1.45	1.65	1.55
85	3.20	3.40	3.50
90	6.00	6.30	6.10
95	9.60	10.00	9.70

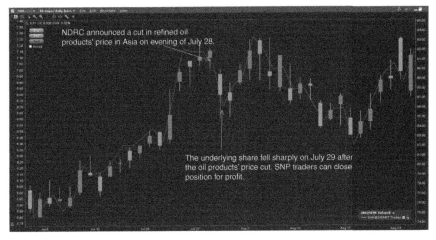

FIGURE 9.2 Price Chart of Sinopec and its ADR
Source: Interactive Brokers LLC.

Traders can anticipate from international oil price movements whether an adjustment in prices is inevitable. Then share prices can best react in response to the magnitude of the price adjustment, as well as the timing in between adjustments.

MAKING ADR PROFITS USING NEWS FROM INSIDE THE UNITED STATES

It is hard for us to imagine that traders in the United States can actually use the news from their own backyard to profit from an ADR with a home market in Asia, but this does happen when an Asian-based company has a significant operation or project in the United States.

Genting Berhad, one of Asia's largest casino operators, had a plan to build the world's largest casino, a US$3.8 billion project with 5,200 hotel rooms, more than 50 restaurants and bars, and a retail shopping mall called Resorts World Miami. However, the plan to build the resort overlooking Miami's Biscayne Bay stalled when a Florida House of Representatives committee postponed a vote on the bill to expand casino gambling on February 3, 2012. Genting had earlier invested some US$500 million buying prime Miami waterfront real estate in anticipation of the project.

Nevertheless, the casino plan required the passage of a destination resort bill. When the bill sponsor, Rep. Erik Fresen, R-Miami, asked that it be temporarily postponed on Friday, February 3, the casino plan was effectively dead for a while and thus the share price of Genting was affected.

Genting Berhad is listed on the Malaysia Stock Exchange. Due to public holidays, the stock market in Malaysia was closed until the following Wednesday, February 8. Traders in the United States who learned about the Florida House of Representatives had plenty of time to take action on the Genting Berhad ADR (GEBHY), which was traded over-the-counter at the Pink OTC Market. However, due to the illiquid nature of the ADR, traders may not have been able to enter into a short trade on it. Nevertheless, the fact that a piece of news on policymaking decisions in the state of Florida could impact the share price of a foreign-listed company created a situation where traders could gain advantage.

Genting's ADR, naturally, did not react much on February 3, 2012, and was trading at US$18.1, or the equivalent of RM10.92 after adjusting for the ADR ratio and foreign exchange. Genting's underlying share closed at RM11.00 on February 3, 2012. When the Malaysian stock market resumed

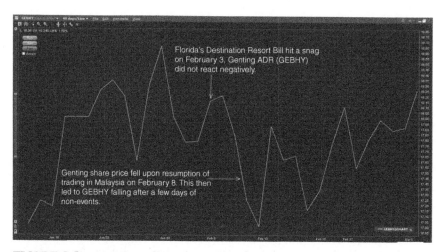

FIGURE 9.3   Price Chart of Genting's ADR
Source: Interactive Brokers LLC.

trading on February 8, Genting's share price dropped significantly to RM10.50 and Genting's ADR also followed suit.

In the future, it will be interesting to see if the Genting ADR will present traders with opportunities to profit, since Genting has plans to have multiple casino and gambling locations in the United States where local governmental decisions on their plans may cause share prices to go up or down, depending on the outcomes.

Figure 9.3 illustrates Genting Berhad's ADR (GEBHY) price action following the Florida Casino Bill being postponed.

SUMMARY

This chapter looked at some case studies involving government policy changes—in both domestic and foreign countries—that could have a price impact on associated companies' ADRs.

The final chapter gives examples of specific company news that can move share prices up or down significantly.

CHAPTER 10

Case Study 4: Material Company-Specific News

B ack in 2007, when the stock market in China was red hot, an issuance of A-shares by existing Chinese companies which were then listed on the Hong Kong Stock Exchange served as a catalyst for a significant price gain.

Information regarding the timetable for the assessment of the A-shares issues by Chinese companies is published on the China Securities Regulatory Commission website (www.csrc.gov.cn). Note, however, that such announcements are only available in the Chinese language section of the website.

During China's equity super bull market period, the share price of companies already listed in Hong Kong (the H-shares) received a big boost when the China Securities Regulatory Commission (CSRC) published its Public Offering Review Committee meeting agenda that contained assessments of associated company's A-shares initial public offerings applications. During that time, the strategy was to buy into companies whose A-shares issuance applications were to be reviewed in the CSRC Public Offering Review working committee meeting. To do that, you have to visit the CSRC website and check the agenda of its working committee meetings, published a few days before the meetings take place. Such a meeting agenda is usually published after the Asian trading hour has closed.

A-SHARES ISSUANCE

As an example, let's look at two Chinese companies' share price performance, when the agenda of the CSRC Public Offering Review working committee meeting to review the respective companies' applications for A-shares issuance were published in September 2007. The two companies are China Shenhua and PetroChina.

China Shenhua

On September 13, 2007, the CSRC published their meeting agenda for the 127th Public Offering Review working committee meeting. The working committee was to be held on September 17, 2007, and the sole agenda was to discuss China Shenhua's A-shares IPO.

Traders who were familiar with the stock market in those days would be expected to buy H-shares of China Shenhua the next day (September 14, 2007). Unfortunately, China Shenhua's ADR was not available in 2007. Nevertheless, this example is just to illustrate that the play in those days was to punt on the expected share price increase that accompanied an A-shares IPO. Table 10.1 illustrates the share-price reaction of China Shenhua when the meeting agenda was first published and after the working committee approved the A-shares IPO on September 17. The trend was that the share price would rise on the expectation that the IPO application would be approved and profit taking would come in after the approval was granted.

PetroChina

On September 20, 2007, the CSRC published the meeting agenda for the135th Public Offering Review working committee meeting. The working committee met on September 24, 2007, and the sole agenda was to review the application of PetroChina's A-shares IPO application.

TABLE 10.1   Share Price Performance of China Shenhua

Date	Share Price	Change (%)	Remark
09/13/2007	38.21	3.49%	The working committee meeting agenda was published after market hours.
09/14/2007	40.19	5.19%	
09/17/2007	39.65	−1.36%	The approval of China Shenhua A-shares IPO released after market closed.
09/18/2007	39.15	−1.25%	

PetroChina's ADR was available then and the ADR ratio was 100 underlying shares for 1 ADR. We could even buy call and put options on this ADR, as it was already an optionable stock. See Table 10.2.

Since the news of the working committee meeting became available after the Asian markets closed, PetroChina's ADR had yet to react and was available at around the same equivalent price as earlier that day in Hong Kong.

You could have bought into PetroChina's ADR at its closing price of US$158.35 as indicated in Table 10.3 on September 20, 2007, and held it overnight. The next day, PetroChina's H-shares listed in Hong Kong surged just under 5 percent to close at HK$12.96. When the U.S. markets opened the next day, you could easily sell it at more than a 5 percent profit as the ADR closed at US$167.22 that day.

However, this scenario includes the background information that a huge price catalyst to PetroChina was occurring during one of China's biggest bull market runs. Thus, a leverage position was justified and you could surely have taken a punt on a PetroChina call option.

Table 10.4 displays PetroChina's ADR call options prices of various strike prices expiring in October 2007 on September 20, 2007. The closing price of PetroChina's ADR on that day was US$158.35. If you expected

TABLE 10.2   Share Price Performance of PetroChina

Date	Share Price	Change (%)	Remark
09/20/2007	12.38	3.51%	The working committee meeting agenda was published after market hours.
09/21/2007	12.96	4.68%	
09/24/2007	14.30	10.34%	The approval of PetroChina A-shares IPO released after market closed.
09/25/2007	13.80	−3.50%	

TABLE 10.3   Price Range of PetroChina Share Price and its ADR Equivalent Price Adjusted for ADR Ratio and Exchange Rate in HK$ on the Days before and after Its A-shares IPO Application Review and Approval

	Actual Underlying Share Price			Equivalent ADR Price (Adjusted) ADR Price in Brackets (US$)		
Date	High	Low	Close	High	Low	Close
09/20/2007	12.54	12.02	12.38	12.24(159.80)	12.02(157.71)	12.12(158.35)
09/21/2007	13.06	12.50	12.96	12.44(167.94)	12.28(165.60)	12.33(167.22)
09/24/2007	14.36	13.14	14.30	13.07(183.74)	12.89(177.74)	13.02(181.12)
09/25/2007	14.28	13.64	13.80	14.28(176.98)	13.82(172.79)	14.08(175.82)

PetroChina's share to rise 5 percent on that piece of news in Hong Kong the next day, you could choose a call option at about 5 percent out-of-the-money that day for a speculative punt. Based on that thinking, you could have chosen either call option with strike prices of US$165 or US$170. If you were most aggressive and went for the US$170 strike, the call option would have cost US$2.90 on September 20, 2007.

On September 21, 2007, after PetroChina underlying share rose 5 percent and the ADR followed suit, the US$170 strike PetroChina call option price rose a staggering 148 percent in one day. Traders who bought this call option would be smiling all the way to the bank. As it turned out, PetroChina's share went through a little phase of irrational exuberance over the next few weeks ahead of its A-share IPO on November 5, 2007. The underlying share almost doubled in the two months and then came crashing down after the A-share made its debut in Shanghai Stock Exchange, as illustrated in Figure 10.1, that shows the price of PetroChina (Stock code: 0857) and its ADR (Symbol: PTR) ahead of its A-share IPO in November 2007.

TABLE 10.4 October 2007 Call Options Prices of PetroChina on September 20, 2007

Strike	Bid	Ask	Last
155	8.50	9.00	9.20
160	5.90	6.40	6.20
165	3.90	4.20	4.30
170	2.55	2.85	2.90

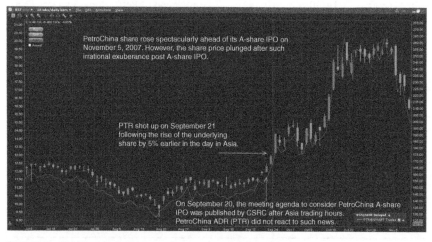

FIGURE 10.1 Price Chart of PetroChina and its ADR

Source: Interactive Brokers LLC.

TABLE 10.5   October 2007 Call Options Prices of PetroChina on September 21, 2007

Strike	Bid	Ask	Last
155	15.60	16.30	15.90
160	12.10	12.80	12.10
165	9.30	9.80	9.40
170	6.90	7.20	7.20

OPERATIONAL STATISTICS

Telecommunication companies like China Unicom announce their operational statistics on a monthly basis to the stock exchange. These disclosures can sometimes have a significant price impact if they indicate a significant milestone for a company.

China Unicom

One such incident took place in June 2010. China Unicom announced its May 2010 operational statistics to the Hong Kong Stock Exchange on June 18, 2010, after the market closed. For the first time, China Unicom was able to achieve its internal target of adding one million new subscribers to its 3G service. This was a significant development, as China Unicom's 3G service had not been well received before it implemented promotions on handsets in May 2010.

This piece of information may only have been useful to investors or traders who were following China Unicom for a while and could understand the implications of such an operational breakthrough. Traders would have needed to be able to correctly interpret the share price impact of such news before taking positions in China Unicom ADR.

After the operational statistics were released, you would have ample time to digest such information since China Unicom's ADR share price barely moved on June 18, 2010. You could have bought China Unicom's ADR at US$12.56 that day and waited for the price to react the next trading day in Hong Kong, Monday, June 21. The underlying share increased 9 percent on Monday and traders who made use of such information to long the ADR on Friday walked home with at least a 6 percent gain.

Once again, you can use call option to enhance your gain when trading on such news. China Unicom's at-the-money (strike price of US$12.50) call option was selling at US$0.50 on June 18, 2010. If you bought this option, you would have made a 100 percent gain as this option doubled to US$1.00 on June 21 after the price reacted to the positive operational data.

TABLE 10.6	Price Range of China Unicom Share Price and its ADR Equivalent Price Adjusted for ADR Ratio and Exchange Rate in HK$ on the Days before and after the Release of Operational Statistics					
	Actual Underlying Share Price			**Equivalent ADR Price (Adjusted) ADR Price in Brackets (US$)**		
Date	High	Low	Close	High	Low	Close
06/17/2010	9.88	9.73	9.79	9.84(12.64)	9.71(12.48)	9.81(12.60)
06/18/2010	9.89	9.54	9.61	9.80(12.59)	9.60(12.34)	9.77(12.56)
06/21/2010	10.62	9.94	10.48	10.56(13.59)	10.27(13.22)	10.38(13.36)

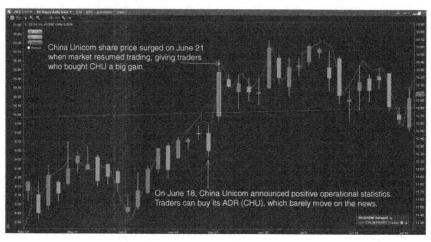

FIGURE 10.2 Price Chart of China Unicom and its ADR

Source: Interactive Brokers LLC.

Figure 10.2 illustrates the price of China Unicom (Stock code: 0762) and its ADR (Symbol: CHU) on the days before and after the release of their operational statistics.

PROFIT ALERTS/WARNINGS

When listed companies anticipate their upcoming financial results to deviate significantly from previous trends, they will typically issue positive profit alerts or negative profit warnings.

As estimates of upcoming profits are normally not anticipated, the share price movement as a result of such announcements can be substantial. Due to its irregular nature, the impact on share price from a positive or negative profit alert may even surpass the release of financial results that are normally well anticipated.

Sinopec Shanghai Petrochemical

Sinopec Shanghai Petrochemical is a company that announces significant changes in profits. The following pages review both a positive profit alert and a profit warning from this company to see how traders can benefit from such news.

On June 10, 2009, Sinopec Shanghai announced to the Hong Kong Stock Exchange that it expected to record a net profit for the first half of 2009 compared to a loss in the same period the previous year. The company attributed the turnaround primarily to a significant drop in raw materials prices and an improved pricing mechanism for refined oil products implemented by the government. This announcement was made after the markets closed in Asia.

Traders who managed to get a hold of this piece of news could take advantage of it by buying into Sinopec Shanghai's ADR. The ADR price barely moved on June 10, 2009 in the United States after the pleasant profit surprise was made known. Sinopec Shanghai's ADR closed at US$33.71 on that day, as indicated on Table 10.7.

The underlying share in Hong Kong surged 7.3 percent the next day as investors reacted to the positive profit alert. When the U.S. market opened on June 11, 2009, the ADR managed to rise 8 percent and handed smart traders a handsome gain.

TABLE 10.7 Price Range of Sinopec Shanghai Petrochemical Share Price and its ADR Equivalent Price Adjusted for ADR Ratio and Exchange Rate in HK$ on the Days before and after the Positive Profit Alert

Date	Actual Underlying Share Price			Equivalent ADR Price (Adjusted) ADR Price in Brackets (US$)		
	High	Low	Close	High	Low	Close
06/09/2009	2.63	2.51	2.55	2.61(33.69)	2.56(33.00)	2.60(33.53)
06/10/2009	2.62	2.57	2.61	2.67(34.50)	2.56(33.01)	2.61(33.71)
06/11/2009	2.87	2.66	2.80	2.85(36.75)	2.77(35.70)	2.82(36.43)

TABLE 10.8   July 2009 Call Options Prices of Sinopec Shanghai on June 10, 2009

Strike	Bid	Ask	Last/Mark
25	8.40	9.10	8.75
30	4.40	5.00	4.70
35	1.65	2.10	1.88
40	0.45	0.70	0.575

TABLE 10.9   July 2009 Call Options Prices of Sinopec Shanghai on June 11, 2009

Strike	Bid	Ask	Last/Mark
25	11.10	12.00	11.55
30	6.60	7.40	7.00
35	3.00	3.70	3.35
40	1.00	1.40	1.20

Those who are familiar with options can even take a punt on Sinopec Shanghai's call option. However, this particular option does not attract much interest and most options are not traded. The prices in Table 10.8 and Table 10.9 illustrate the call option prices of Sinopec Shanghai's ADR on June 10 at the close, with the bid and ask as well as the last traded or mark-to-market prices.

Traders who chose to buy Sinopec Shanghai's ADR slightly out-of-money call option with a strike price of US$35 on June 10 at a price of US$1.88 would have achieved a profit of close to 80 percent assuming the option was liquidated the next day at US$3.35. This is quite a remarkable return for one day's work!

Figure 10.3 illustrates the price of Sinopec Shanghai (Stock code: 0338) and its ADR (Symbol: SHI) on the days before and after the positive profit alert.

Besides providing traders with a chance to profit from a positive price alert, Sinopec Shanghai also provided opportunities for traders to make money from profit warnings they issued to the stock exchange.

On January 18, 2012, after the stock market closed in Hong Kong, Sinopec Shanghai Petrochemical Company Limited told the Hong Kong Exchange that its net profit for the financial year ending December 2011 would be 50 to 70 percent lower than 2010 based on its finance department's preliminary estimates.

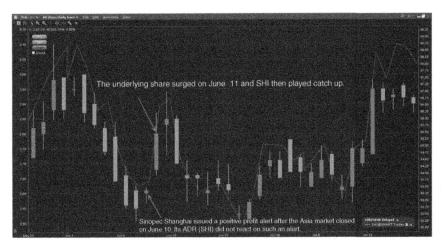

FIGURE 10.3 Price Chart of Sinopec Shanghai and its ADR

Source: Interactive Brokers LLC.

It is obvious from the price action that, unlike its parent company Sinopec—which was sure to attract attention—Sinopec Shanghai's ADR did not react to such negative news and its share price was actually up on January 18, in line with a strong day in the U.S. market. The ADR actually rose slightly that day to US$38.92, as indicated in Table 10.10.

Traders who were alerted to the profit warning would have been able to short Sinopec Shanghai's ADR on January 18 at US$38.92. On January 19, Sinopec Shanghai's share price in Hong Kong dropped 4.7 percent and the ADR then reacted and fell to US$36.84.

Options traders could have bought the slightly in-the-money put option with a strike price of US$40.00 on January 18 for a price of US$2.35. On

TABLE 10.10	Price Range of Sinopec Shanghai Petrochemical Share Price and its ADR Equivalent Price Adjusted for ADR Ratio and Exchange Rate in HK$ on the Days before and after the Profit Warning					

	Actual Underlying Share Price			**Equivalent ADR Price (Adjusted) ADR Price in Brackets (US$)**		
Date	**High**	**Low**	**Close**	**High**	**Low**	**Close**
01/17/2012	3.02	2.95	3.00	3.01(38.76)	2.97(38.25)	2.98(38.33)
01/18/2012	3.03	2.93	2.97	3.05(39.26)	2.94(37.91)	3.02(38.92)
01/19/2012	2.95	2.81	2.83	2.92(37.67)	2.85(36.71)	2.86(36.84)

the next day, this option would return more than 50 percent to those who bought it the day before, as shown in Tables 10.11 and 10.12.

Figure 10.4 illustrates the price of Sinopec Shanghai (Stock code: 0338) and its ADR (Symbol: SHI) on the days before and after the profit warning.

TABLE 10.11 February 2012 Put Options Prices of Sinopec Shanghai on January 18, 2012

Strike	Bid	Ask	Last/Mark
30	0	0.45	0.225
35	0.20	0.80	0.95
40	2.00	2.70	2.35
45	5.60	6.80	6.20

TABLE 10.12 February 2012 Put Options Prices of Sinopec Shanghai on January 19, 2012

Strike	Bid	Ask	Last/Mark
30	0	0.50	0.225
35	0.55	1.30	0.95
40	3.20	4.20	3.70
45	7.50	8.70	8.10

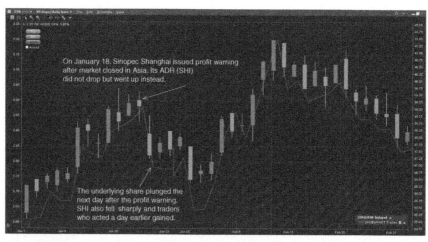

FIGURE 10.4   Price Chart of Sinopec Shanghai and its ADR

Source: Interactive Brokers LLC.

SUMMARY

This final chapter offers case studies on company-specific news from domestic market IPOs to profit alerts or warnings and the impacts they can have on share price movements.

The last four chapters offered many examples from the past to validate the concept of making relatively easy profits using news and information from after-hour news in Asian markets.

After reading through this whole book, you should be convinced that there are, indeed, free lunches in the stock market provided you know how to look for them. This also means that the stock market is not very efficient despite the availability of online news and sophisticated trading systems.

This book is written for the average retail investor who is adventurous enough to trade foreign shares using ADRs. While trading foreign markets may be viewed as difficult for many, this book shows that this may not necessarily be the case. Getting ahead of the pack always enhances making money in the stock market. This book tells you how you can gain that trading edge by using tomorrow's news.

Many people like to trade conventional stocks or instruments. While this may be the easier or safer way to dabble in the stock market, in that area you are dealing with many more knowledgeable investors, such as fund managers and institutions. ADRs seem like exotic things and many investors may think that these instruments are not for them to trade. However, you may actually be able to make better money on them because not that many people are in the game. The liquidity in ADRs may not be attractive for big institutional funds and because of that a small retail investor has a chance to succeed at trading ADRs.

We already showed you how you can look for the trading edge required to make money from ADRs, so why hesitate?

Start by opening a brokerage account that allows you to trade both exchange-traded and over-the-counter ADRs and start your journey to making money with confidence!

The Art of Decoding the Earnings Announcement

By Paul Lau
Certified Public Accountant[1]

Alongside the main chapters about the ADRs of listed companies, you may find this Appendix concerning the ways of decoding the earnings announcement (using just addition, subtraction, and division) of a listed company useful. This Appendix also tells the story behind the mathematics for decoding an earnings announcement, such as ratio analysis and calculating the PE ratio and EPS.

THE TWO EQUATIONS

Before reading further, there are two equations that you should understand:

1. Assets – Liabilities = Owner's equity
2. Cash Flow = Cash from Operations + Cash from Investing Activities + Cash from Financing Activities

---

[1]Professional designation: UK: Fellow Member of Association of Chartered Certified Accountant ACCA. HK: Fellow Member/Practising Certificate Holder of Hong Kong Institute of Certified Public Accountants.

These two equations are keystones for you to understand:

1. The capital structure of the company.
2. The way of earning for the period under review.
3. The management of the cash flows of the listed company for the period under review.

Further to these two equations, the listed company presents its financial data in the form of the set of financial statements, known as the annual report. The annual report of a listed company usually consists of the following components:

1. Chairman statement.
2. Information on stock options and others.
3. Auditors' report.
4. Income statement.
5. Statement of comprehensive income.
6. Statement of changes in owner's equity.
7. Statement of financial position (in the past, we called this the balance sheet).
8. Statement of cash flows.
9. Notes to financial statements.
10. Summary of the past five years' business results.

Indeed, the preceding 10 items are then subdivided into the following parts:

Quantitative understanding: Items 4 and 7 belong to this first part. Let us do some ratio analysis on these statements. By the end of this, you should know more about the performance of the listed company during the period under review.

Qualitative understanding: Items 1 to 3, 5 to 6, and 8 to 10 belong to this second part.

Items 1 and 3 are especially important to understand whether the company is a going concern (how the listed company is doing currently). It also provides a foundation of what is needed to study a stock price for a listed company

I will not go into the details of items 2 and 10. All the past information of a listed company should be well reflected in its stock price. Therefore, stock option information and the summary of five years' financials are available for you to better your understanding of the stock price.

Other parts are quite long but I introduce some parts here about how a stock price performs in the open market, including:

- Doing ratio analysis (pure mathematics).
- Understanding the quantitative and qualitative items (the story behind the pure mathematics, i.e., ratio analysis).

The following external factors are important in reviewing the annual report, and you should always bear them in mind when reading one. They are:

- Exchange rate
- Interest rate
- Inflation
- Issue of government

Exchange rate, interest rate, and inflation are the indicators that we use to measure the true value (such as, market value, intrinsic value, or real purchasing power) of a listed company. I won't go into details on these factors, as many other finance books are available for you if you want to get more background for yourself.

Currently, the influence of government policy is quite a big matter to the business community. The European crisis originated from the overreliance of financing through government bonds in either the short run or long run, placing a heavy burden on Europe (i.e., cuts to government spending and increased taxes on citizens and corporations). In addition, the credit rating downgrades of the U.S. government led to rising costs for borrowing in the United States. These actions are not good (i.e., sharp increases in taxes or interest rates) and decrease the net earnings to listed companies during the period under review.

External factors are a must to take into consideration when decoding the earnings announcement affecting the real value of the listed company, its net margin, and dividend policy.

Here is an example to illustrate the principles I have mentioned so far. For easy reference, an income statement (Table A.1) and a statement of financial position (Table A.2) found on pp. 144–145.

For illustration purposes, no other components of the financial statements except for Tables A.1 and A.2 are shown in the following discussions and calculations.

TABLE A.1 KP Zoo Limited Consolidated Income Statement for the Year Ending December 31, 2010

	2010 US$ Million	2009 US$ Million
Revenue	209,180	208,808
Costs of goods sold	(78,321)	(74,275)
Staff costs	(28,768)	(28,309)
Depreciation and amortization	(14,932)	(16,258)
Change in fair value of investment properties	855	1,117
Profit on disposal of investment	–	12,472
Other operating expenses	(50,618)	(68,246)
	37,396	35,309
Interest and other finance costs	(8,476)	(9,613)
Profit before tax	28,920	25,696
Current tax	(2,493)	(4,588)
Deferred tax	(847)	92
Profit after tax and attributable to shareholders	25,580	21,200
Earnings per share for profit attributable to ordinary shareholders of the company	US$4.65	US$3.85

Let us get back to a closer look on the two equations mentioned in the beginning of this Appendix. The first of the two equations states Assets − Liabilities = owner's equity and the answer is easily found in Table A.2.

As demonstrated for the year ending December 31, 2010:

Assets = Non-Current Assets + Current Assets ($554,563 + $166,614) = $721,177

Liabilities = Current Liabilities + Non-Current Liabilities ($106,911 + $261,564) = $368,475

Assets − Liabilities ($721,177 − $368,475) = $352,702 (i.e., owner's equity)

TABLE A.2	KP Zoo Limited Consolidated Statement of Financial Position for the Year Ending December 31, 2010	

ASSETS	2010 US$ Million	2009 US$ Million
Non-current assets		
Fixed assets	167,851	176,192
Investment properties	43,240	42,323
Leasehold land	27,561	29,191
Goodwill	27,332	28,858
Brand names and other rights	12,865	7,351
Other noncurrent assets	251,129	225,977
Liquid funds and other listed investments	24,585	23,213
	554,563	533,105
Current assets		
Cash and cash equivalents	91,652	92,521
Trade and other receivables	57,229	48,146
Inventories	17,733	16,593
	166,614	157,260
Current liabilities		
Trade and other payables	80,889	73,029
Bank and other debts	23,122	17,589
Current tax liabilities	2,900	3,249
	106,911	93,867
Net current assets	59,703	63,393
Non-current liabilities		
Bank and other debts	228,134	242,851
Interest bearing loans from noncontrolling shareholders	13,493	13,424
Deferred tax liabilities	14,290	13,355
Other noncurrent liabilities	5,647	6,956
	261,564	276,586
Net assets	352,702	319,912
CAPITAL AND RESERVES		
Share capital	1,066	1,066
Reserves	308,431	281,433
	309,497	282,499
Noncontrolling interests*	43,205	37,413
	352,702	319,912

*The noncontrolling interests represent the share of net assets on subsidiaries by the investors whose ownerships are insignificant relative to the total number of outstanding shares of subsidiaries.

You can induce more insights from the above calculations, as follows:

- Noncurrent assets were about 76.9 percent (=$554,563/$721,177) of the total assets of the KP Zoo Limited.

- Current assets were able to repay the current liabilities but short of paying noncurrent liabilities, unless some noncurrent assets were sold to cover that position.

- The funding for KP Zoo Limited on the acquisition of the assets was approximately contributed by 51 percent (=$368,475/$721,177) from all creditors and 49 percent (=$352,702/$721,177) from the shareholders.

Further, the major points for understanding the capital structure of KP Zoo Limited as of December 31, 2010, are stated as:

- How much is invested in the noncurrent assets of KP Zoo Limited for the continuing of business operations in the coming future.

- Creditors' funds are the major source of financing of KP Zoo Limited.

- If the management of KP Zoo Limited intends to extend its business operations, creditor's financing, or placement offer to the existing shareholders, it should be carefully structured to avoid any conflict or dispute in between.

By understanding the capital structure of KP Zoo Limited, you may seek to know more about its cash flows in order to evaluate the stock price.

In Table A.3, a statement of cash flows is presented in extract form for easy demonstration of the management of cash flows for KP Zoo Limited.

Let's now look at the second part of the two equations:

Cash flows = cash from/(used in) operations + cash from/(used in) investing activities + cash from/(used in) financing activities

The second part of the two equations, in accordance with the data as shown in Table A.3, is performed this way:

Cash flows of KP Zoo Limited = cash from operations

+cash (used in) from financing activities

+cash from (used in) financing activities

= $29,867 + ($31,536) + $800

= ($869) (i.e., decreasing cash balances for year 2010)

| **TABLE A.3** | KP Zoo Limited Consolidated Statement of Cash Flows (Extract) for the Year Ending December 31, 2010 |

Operating activities	2010 US$ Million	2009 US$ Million
Cash generated from operating activities	43,262	36,517
Interest paid and other finance costs paid	(7,763)	(8,910)
Tax paid	(2,617)	(2,866)
	32,882	24,741
Changes in working capital	(3,015)	(4,514)
Net cash from operations	**29,867**	**20,227**
Investing activities		
Purchases of fixed assets	(21,683)	(19,052)
Additions to leasehold land	(54)	(30)
Additions to brand names and other rights	(461)	(494)
Purchase of subsidiary companies	–	(126)
Proceeds on disposal of subsidiary companies	(69)	15,892
Additions on other noncurrent assets	(8,565)	13,916
	(30,832)	10,106
Disposals of liquid funds & other listed investments	523	13,468
Additions to liquid funds & other listed investments	(1,227)	(4,835)
Cash flows (used in) from investing activities	**(31,536)**	**18,739**
Financing activities		
New borrowings	41,232	111,452
Repayments of borrowings	(49,434)	(103,182)
Issue of shares by subsidiary companies to noncontrolling shareholders	23,569	(487)
Payments to acquire additional interests in subsidiary companies	(4,727)	(610)
Dividends paid to noncontrolling shareholders	(2,465)	(3,529)
Dividends paid to ordinary shareholders	(7,375)	(7,375)

(continues)

TABLE A.3	KP Zoo Limited Consolidated Statement of Cash Flows (Extract) for the Year Ending December 31, 2010 *(continued)*

Operating activities	2010 US$ Million	2009 US$ Million
Cash flows from (used in) financing activities	800	(3,731)
(Decrease) Increase in cash and cash equivalents	(869)	35,235
Cash and cash equivalent at 1 January	92,521	57,286
Cash and cash equivalents at 31 December	<u>91,652</u>	<u>92,521</u>

Again, inducing from Table A.3 on the cash flows of KP Zoo Limited on December 31, 2010:

- Cash and cash equivalents were decreasing from \$92,521 to \$91,652 during the year 2010.
- Various funding from financing activities and net cash from operations were almost used to cover spending in investing activities.
- Dividends paid to noncontrolling shareholders/ordinary shareholders were different.

Further, the major observations to be made upon reviewing the cash flows of KP Zoo Limited at December 31, 2010, are:

- The management of KP Zoo Limited have a well-balanced strategy on the control of cash flows during year 2010. The cash position is slightly decreased but still keeping at a good position for \$91,652 million (i.e., 25.9 percent of the net assets).
- No change is noted in the dividend policy for ordinary shareholders. However, this may be a good indication of stock price or vice versa. No matter how good KP Zoo Limited is at achieving in future periods, the fixed payout dividends ratio to ordinary shareholders would be unpleasant. Or in a recession, a fixed dividend payout ratio may be a gift to the ordinary shareholders. This is a complex signal on the analysis of stock price.

By understanding the cash flows of KP Zoo Limited, you may find insight about what the management has done to maintain its capital structure.

The ways they manage surplus funds from operations covers the shortfall in cash used in investing activities for year 2010.

So far the two equations should give you a better understanding of the results of KP Zoo Limited for year 2010 on a macro perspective. In terms of a micro perspective, we can do a quick scan of the health of KP Zoo Limited by using quantitative understanding and qualitative understanding for year 2010.

Thus, to review the micro perspective:

- Do the pure mathematics (ratio analysis).
- Read the chairman's statement.
- Read the auditor's report.
- Read the notes to financial statements.

After these steps, you will have collected a bundle of performance indicators and useful information about how the business of KP Zoo Limited has done so far.

Let us begin by doing the pure mathematics (i.e., the quantitative understanding) of the earnings announcement of KP Zoo Limited. Strictly speaking, this section is a bit mechanical and boring in the sense that you just look up figures and plug them into formulas for ratio analysis. In the context of ratio analysis, there are several folds, which are presented as follows:

Investment valuation ratio

- P/E ratio = stock price (quoted in open market)/Earning per share (EPS)
- Dividend yield = Dividend (per share)/stock price

Liquidity measurement ratio

- Working capital ratio = Current assets (CA)/Current Liabilities (CL)
- Quick ratio = (CA – Inventory)/CL

Profitability indicator ratio

- Profit margin = Net profits/Net sales
- Operating margin = Operating income/Net sales
- Return on equity = (Net profits – Dividends to preferred shareholders)/Owner's equity
- Effective tax rate = Income tax/Profit before tax

Financial leverage ratio

- Interest coverage = EBIT (Earnings before interest and tax)/Interest expense
- Debt to equity ratio = Total debts/Owner's equity
- Long-term debts to net working capital = Noncurrent debts/(CA – CL)

Operating performance ratio

- Inventory turnover = Costs of goods sold/Average inventory for the period
- Fixed assets turnover = Net sales/Net fixed assets
- Accounts receivable turnover = Net sales/Average gross receivable

These selected ratios allow you to have a quick look on the performance edge of the management of funds for a listed company during the period under review. Generally, ratio analyses are calculated for the purpose of evaluating aspects of a listed company's operations and fall into the following categories:

- Investment valuation ratios measure the market price relative to the listed company's earnings and dividends.
- Liquidity measurement ratios measure a listed company's ability to meet its current obligations.
- Profitability indicator ratios measure the efficiency on the profit derived from the operations.
- Financial leverage ratios measure the degree of protection of long-term debts, the listed company's ability to raise additional debt, and its capacity to pay its liabilities on a repayment schedule.
- Operating performance ratios measure the efficiency of the business turnover achieved as to the assets invested by the listed company over the periods.

SUMMARY OF RATIO ANALYSES

Let's begin the ratio analyses and summarize the results of the preceding statements for KP Zoo Limited.

The results of the following ratios are based on the data shown in Tables A.1 and A.2. In addition, we assume that the stock price to be US$10.19 for year 2010 and US$6.75 for year 2009, respectively, and dividend per share to be US$1.34 for years 2010 and 2009.

Investment Valuation Ratio

	Calculation	2010	2009	Calculation
P/E ratio	10.19/4.65	2.19	1.75	6.75/3.85
Dividend yield	1.34/10.19	13.15%	19.85%	1.34/6.75

Liquidity Measurement Ratio

	Calculation	2010	2009	Calculation
Working capital ratio	166,614/106,911	1.56	1.68	157,260/93,867
Quick ratio	(166,614 − 17,733)/106,911	1.39	1.50	(157,260 − 16,593)/93,867

Profitability Indicator Ratio

	Calculation	2010	2009	Calculation
Profit margin	25,580/209,180	12.22%	10.15%	21,200/208,808
Operating margin	37,396/209,180	17.87%	16.9%	35,309/208,808
Return on equity	(25,580 − 0)/352,702	7.25%	6.63%	(21,200 − 0)/319,912
Effective tax rate	(2,493+847)/28,920	11.5%	17.5%	(4,588 − 92)/25,696

Financial Leverage Ratio

Interest coverage

2010: 37,396/8,476 = 4.41

2009: 35,309/9,613 = 3.67

Debt-to-equity ratio

2010: (23,122+228,134+13,493+5,647)/352,702 = 0.77

2009: (17,589+242,851+13,424+6,956)/319,912 = 0.88

Long-term debts to net working capital

2010: (228,134+13,493+5,647)/(166,614 − 106,911) = 4.14

2009: (242,851+13,424+6,956)/(157,260–93,867) = 4.15

Operating Performance Ratio

Inventory turnover

2010: 78,321/[(16,593+17,733)/2] = 4.56

2009: 74,275/[(18,528+16,593)/2] = 4.23

Fixed assets turnover

2010: 209,180/167,851 = 1.25

2009: 208,808/176,192 = 1.19

Account receivable turnover

Assuming the trade receivable (gross) was $30,484 in 2010 and $29,081 in 2009:

2010: 209,180/30,484 = 6.86

2009: 208,808/29,081 = 7.18

Comparative ratios are calculated for the year 2009 in Table A.4 so we have an understanding of the trends of various financial areas. Before going into the details of various ratio analyses, two more simple ratios are also calculated for this discussion: growth in net sales and depreciation as a percentage on net sales.

Let's assume the net sales in 2008 were $235,478 million.

Growth/Drop in net sales

2010: (209,180 − 208,808)/208,808 = increase of 0.178 percent

2009: (208,808 − 235,478)/235,478 = decrease of 11.32 percent

Depreciation as a percentage on net sales

2010: 14,932/209,180 = 0.071

2009: 16,258/208,808 = 0.077

Based on the above ratio analyses, the results of KP Zoo Limited during the years 2010 and 2009 are summarized as follows:

- The sales of 2010 and 2009 were not as good as those of 2008.
- For every dollar made in sales, $0.071 (2009: $0.077) was paid as a contribution to fixed assets invested over the years.
- The PE ratio slightly increased from 1.75 to 2.19. This indicates the stock traded at a premium in the open market of 2009. Investors expect KP Zoo Limited will continue its success. However, the dividend yield is not good, as it drops from 19.85 to 13.15 percent. The

amount of dividends paid to ordinary shareholders remains unchanged at $7,375 million (see Table A.3). The stock price increased from $6.75 to $10.19 since 2009. Investors feel that dividend yield is unattractive as it is diluted by its open market value.

- Liquidity ratios show that current liabilities are well covered by the level of current assets.
- Profitability indicator ratios are favorable in 2010, as they show an increase in the margin level on sales and the return on equity. Further, the effective tax rate is improved by a lower tax rate, from 17.5 to 11.5 percent.
- Financial leverage ratios show that the interest/debts levels are well covered by its earnings and the contribution by ordinary shareholders.
- For the operating performance ratio, the results are contradictory. Turnovers on inventory and fixed assets drop and the receivable turnover increases from 2009.

After carefully studying the results of ratio analysis for KP Zoo Limited, you may realize certain principles that are worth reviewing about the earnings announcement, including:

- The ratios of working capital are indicators of the short-term solvency of a listed company and in determining if a listed company can pay its current liabilities when due.
- The ratios on profitability indicators measure the ability of a listed company to create profits from its assets.
- The financial leverage ratio is a good indicator of the listed company's ability to protect creditors in case of insolvency, meet interest payments, and pay long-term debt from current assets after paying current liabilities.
- An operating performance ratio leads us to understand the liquidity of the listed company's receivables and inventory, and their utilization with aid from the quality of fixed assets.
- The PE ratio/dividend yield is an indicator of the open market's reaction to the listed company's EPS and dividend policy.

After this heavy exercise on ratio analysis, we then read the chairman's report and the auditors' report—the qualitative understanding portion of our analysis.

All the existing business developments, prospects and new plans of acquisition (at time during economic downturn, disposals of non-core business operations) are laid out in these two reports for readers. Such information is important for readers who are interested in:

1. The evaluation of the stock price.
2. The estimation of future trends for the stock price.

Usually, the chairman's report contains the following components:

a. An introducing paragraph about the listed company's business operations with emphasis on the growth of revenue and EBIT.
b. A discussion of the profits attributable to ordinary shareholders and the EPS, together with matters on the revaluation that affect the earnings during the period.
c. The announcement of final dividend.
d. Information on the established business (i.e., geographical considerations and the market in each established business).
e. The outlook paragraph that discusses:
    1. The business strategy of the development of established businesses.
    2. The possible acquisition of new businesses.,
    3. The disposals of noncore business.
    4. The reorganization of existing corporate structure for cost-control purposes in order to strengthen the growth in EBIT and enhance the payments of dividends to the ordinary shareholders.

By reading the above components of the chairman's report for a listed company, investors may find insight on what the direction of the established business will be, as well as the possible movement of the stock price in an open market.

Let us switch our attention to a discussion of the auditor's report in conjunction with the chairman's report. This is an important part of qualitative understanding—how the books and records of a listed company are prepared in order to present its financial results and the EPS for the period under review. Usually, the auditor's report is divided into the following paragraphs:

• An introductory paragraph presenting the review the sets of financial statements that include:
    1. The income statement.
    2. Statement of comprehensive of income.
    3. Statement of changes in owner's equity.

4. Statement of financial position.

5. Statement of cash flows for the period under review.

- A paragraph on the director's responsibility for the preparation of financial statements.

- A paragraph on the auditor's responsibility for the audit on financial statements.

- A paragraph on the basis for qualified opinion (if required).

- A paragraph on the audit opinion formed on the financial statements (either in clean opinion or with modified opinion).

In fact, the reader should take a closer look at the third paragraph in the auditor's report compared to the first two paragraphs. The auditor's opinion is created with all the information and books and records made available for the auditor's examination in order to form an opinion as to:

a. A true and fair view.

b. Modifications to the auditor's opinion.

A true and fair view represents that the auditor is satisfied on all the available information, and books and records reflect the true position of the balances for the period under review. However, if a modification to the auditor's opinion is made, this means:

- *The auditor concludes that, based on the audit evidence obtained, the financial statements as a whole are not free from material misstatement; or*

- *The auditor is unable to obtain sufficient appropriate audit evidence to conclude that the financial statements as a whole are free from material misstatement.*[2]

Hence, the auditor's report, in either the form of true and fair view or in modification, leads the reader to consider whether the books and records (or financial statements) are truly recorded in order to rely on the evaluation for a correct quantitative understanding.

Table A.4 includes the summaries of some examples of what the modifications to the auditor's opinions look like:

Readers (i.e., investors) of the annual report should bear in mind when looking at the auditor's opinion (toward overall consideration of the

---

[2]Hong Kong Institute of Certified Public Accountants Member's Handbooks, *HKSA 705 (Clarified) Modifications to the Opinion in the Independent Auditor's Report.*

TABLE A.4 Examples of Modifications to the Auditor's Opinions

Listed Company in HKEx*	Code	Financial Period	Reasons for Modification of Auditor's Opinion
Ngai Lik Industrial Holdings Limited	332	March 31, 2011	Emphasis was made on the material uncertainty that might cast significant doubt to continue as a going concern.
Climax International Company Limited	439	March 31, 2011	Qualified opinion was made due to the loss of accounting books and records of subsidiary companies.
China Rails media Corporation Limited	745	March 31, 2011	Disclaimer of opinion was made due to the material uncertainty and inability to obtain sufficient appropriate audit evidence relating to recoverability of other receivable and arbitration.
China Environmental Energy Investment Limited ("the Group")	986	March 31, 2011	Disclaimer of opinion was made that the opening balances of the Group's assets, liabilities, and accumulated losses were unable to determine if they were accurately recorded and accounted for due to a disclaimer opinion issued in last year.

*Extracts of information from the annual reports of listed companies in the Hong Kong Stock Exchange. (www.hkexnews.hk/index.htm). The above selected auditor's reports of the listed companies are only for illustration purposes to show modifications to audit opinions. No expression of any adverse opinion is intended for any of the listed companies.

direction for the established business), what the possible movements of the stock price in the open market will be.

The last component in the micro perspective is qualitative understanding. The review includes notes to the financial statements of a listed company done in order to know what the business operations look like.

Usually notes to financial statements are divided into the following categories:

- Corporation information.
- Summary of significant accounting policies.
- Adoption of new or amended financial reporting standards.
- Critical accounting estimates and judgements.
- Details on business operations.
- Breakdowns on the balances:.
    1. The income statement.
    2. Statement of financial position.

- Summaries of:
  1. Capital commitments.
  2. Corporate guarantees.
  3. Contingency due to arbitration/or litigation.
- Summary of related party transactions.
- Summary of five years results.

Hence, certain areas can be selected to continue the study, including:

- Details of the business operations, such as segment reporting.
- Breakdowns of the balances in statements of financial position, such as the lead schedule for fixed assets (i.e., property, plant and equipment), trade and other receivables, and borrowings and other debts.
- Capital commitment and contingency considerations as an element for evaluating the long-term effect on the results of the earnings/stock price of a listed company.

The primary objective of selecting these areas is to review current business achievements and formulate some forecasts about what else can affect the results of the listed company in the future.

SEGMENT REPORTING

Segment reporting consists of detailed analyses of the listed company's revenue, EBIT, capital expenditure, total assets, depreciation and amortization, and total liabilities into two categories: established business and geographical location.

See Table A.5 for an example of a segment information report.

When looking at the extract of operating segment information for KP Zoo Limited for the year ending December 31, 2010, the results are quite contradictory. Tables A.6 and A.7 summarize.

These tables show the revenue and EBIT of KP Zoo Limited exhibited an upward movement. On one hand, the parts within the segment of either established business or geographical location demonstrate downward movement on either revenue or contribution to EBIT. On the other hand, new business makes an additional contribution to revenue or a certain sector's results drastically change to cover the heavy losses incurred from last year.

TABLE A.5	KP Zoo Limited Operating Segment Information (Extract) for the Year Ending December 31, 2010

	Revenue			
Established Business	**2010 US$ Million**	**%**	**2009 US$ Million**	**%**
Ports and related services	32,720	16%	29,492	14%
Property and hotels	5,682	2%	5,233	3%
Retails	102,014	49%	96,552	46%
KP Infrastructure	2,997	1%	2,404	1%
HY Energy	45,213	22%	–	–
KP Telecommunications	16,432	8%	71,538	34%
Others	4,122	2%	3,589	2%
	209,180	100%	208,808	100%

	EBIT			
Geographical Location	**2010 US$ Million**	**%**	**2009 US$ Million**	**%**
Hong Kong	11,736	31%	13,317	38%
Mainland China	11,028	29%	14,043	40%
Asia and Australia	5,072	14%	7,451	21%
Europe	7,505	20%	(2,937)	(8%)
Americas and Others	2,055	6%	3,435	9%
	37,396	100%	35,309	100%

TABLE A.6	Summary for Revenue by Established Business

Established Business	**Particulars**	**Trend as Compared to Last Year**
Revenue	Increased from $208,808 to $209,180.	Increased 0.178% from last year.
Retail	Remains the core business for KP Zoo Limited for 2010 (49%) and 2009 (46%).	Increased 5.66% from last year.
HY Energy	New business started in 2010.	Contributed 22% to KP Zoo's revenue in 2010, 2nd place in overall % contribution.
KP Telecom	Dropped from $71,538 to $16,432.	Decreased 77.03% from last year.

TABLE A.7 Summary for EBIT by Geographical Location

Geographical Location	Particulars	Trend as Compared to Last Year
EBIT	Increased from $35,309 to $37,396	Increased 5.91% from last year.
Hong Kong	Remains the largest contributor of EBIT to KP Zoo Limited in 2010.	However, the EBIT in this sector decreased 11.9% from last year.
Mainland China	Dropped to 2nd place for the contribution of EBIT to KP Zoo Limited in year 2010.	EBIT decreased 21.5% from last year.
Europe	This sector remains in 3rd place for its contribution in 2010. However, it has improved a lot, changing from a negative contribution to a positive contribution of EBIT.	EBIT increased 355% from last year.
Overall	Except for EBIT contribution in Europe, all others are dropping from last year.	n/a

Overall, segment reporting contains very important messages for readers to use when considering how the business is operating for a listed company.

BREAKDOWNS ON BALANCES

Reading the breakdowns of fixed assets, trade and other receivables, and borrowing and other debts are imperative when studying the movements and balances recorded in an income statement, a statement of comprehensive income, and a statement of changes in owner equity.

For a lead schedule of fixed assets, certain data are worth looking at to find out what is behind them. For example, the market value of investment properties and the depreciation on fixed assets should be recorded in the statement of comprehensive income and income statement respectively. By reading the results of the revaluation from investment properties or the depreciation of fixed assets, readers can find out how much has been contributed to current earnings or how much earnings has been eroded by the increase in depreciation of fixed assets.

For a lead schedule of trade and other receivables, things like data, gross receivables, impairment loss on doubtful debts and other receivables, are usually shown. Table A.8 shows a review of such data.

TABLE A.8   KP Zoo Limited trade and Other Receivables at December 31, 2010

Items	2010 US$ Million	2009 US$ Million
Trade receivables—gross	30,484	29,081
Less: Provision for estimated impairment losses for bad debts	(5,563)	(5,852)
Trade receivables—net	24,921	23,229
Other receivables and prepayments	32,308	24,917
	57,229	48,146

TABLE A.9   KP Zoo Limited—Borrowings and Other Debts (All in US$ Million)

Items	Current	Noncurrent	2010	Current	Noncurrent	2009
Bank loans	14,357	83,432	97,789	8,688	88,576	97,264
Other loans	188	441	629	526	426	952
Bonds	8,577	144,261	152,838	8,375	153,849	162,224
	23,122	228,134	251,256	17,589	242,851	260,440

TABLE A.10   KP Zoo Limited—Borrowings and Other Debts by Fair Values (All in US$ Million)

Items	Carrying Value		Fair Value	
	2010	2009	2010	2009
Bank loans	97,395	96,930	97,395	96,925
Other loans	571	952	568	949
Bonds	153,290	162,558	161,699	169,345
	251,256	260,440	259,662	267,219

The figures on the provision for estimated impairment losses for bad debts line show that the management of KP Zoo Limited considers 18.2 percent (i.e., $5,563/$30,484) in 2010 and 20.1 percent (i.e., $5,852/$29,081) in 2009 to be estimated impairment loss on bad debts. That means that a difference of US$289 million has been written back in the income statement as a contribution to current earnings of KP Zoo Limited in 2010. From this data, we realize that additional earnings may arise from the written back item in trade and other receivables.

This example helps us better understand how the management of trade receivables enhances the earnings of a listed company

For lead schedules of borrowing and other debts, information on borrowings is mostly presented as shown in Tables A.9, A.10, and A.11.

TABLE A.11 KP Zoo Limited—Borrowings and Other Debts by Currencies (All in US$ Million)

Borrowings at Principal Amount Denominated in Following Currencies	2010 Percentage	2009 Percentage
HK dollars	31%	30%
US dollars	29%	31%
Euro	28%	28%
British pounds	5%	5%
Other currencies	7%	6%
	100%	100%

Based on these three tables, certain external factors mentioned earlier in this appendix are relevant to the evaluation of borrowings and other debts.

For instance, if there is a change in Euro exchange rates, 28 percent of our debts denominated in Euro will be affected. If the Euro goes up, more U.S. dollars are needed to repay such debts. Such actions will bring changes in exchange loss and a shortage of cash flows. Thus, additional exchange losses will be shown in the income statement and the statement of cash flows will show the additional repayment, too.

Also, if interest rates go up, it will affect both carrying values and fair values of all of the debts. The technique of doing a fair value on debts is not discussed here in order to avoid complex finance theory and time value calculations. Also, if borrowing costs increase it would be shown as an additional finance cost in the income statement.

So, basically, changes due to external factors affect things such as:

1. The carrying values of debts in the statement of financial position.
2. The borrowing costs/exchange loss in an income statement.
3. Cash used for repaying debts.

CAPITAL COMMITMENT AND CONTINGENCY

Capital commitment concentrates on the spending contracted for, or authorized but not contracted for, the coming year. As this appendix has presented, the annual report of a listed company usually lays out the details about how much is to be spent in the future. This information leads us to think about whether this will affect:

1. The drop in dividend-payout ratio due to additional capital spending.
2. The cut in employees' remunerations in order to achieve automation of production lines (i.e., replacing the workers by automated robots/ machines).

Thus, capital commitments do make an impact on future earnings.

Contingency represents a potential liability that might become an actual liability and a loss. Indeed, in a contingency, a listed company provides that any kind of corporate guarantees made during the ordinary course of business, as well as any arbitration or litigation where a settlement is uncertain at the date of its reporting and which may become an actual liability, makes it as if the arrangement is broken. This section indicates that the contingent liability is possible and the listed company's earnings or cash flows may be affected by additional claims by a party of concern.

The contingency accepts that a company's financial position can be affected by heavy consumption in capital assets or by unexpected cash outlays for claims.

TYPICAL PITFALLS IN THE EARNINGS ANNOUNCEMENT

In order to build assumptions and evaluations about the health of a listed company, we discussed a method for evaluating the quantitative and qualitative areas of an annual report.

By using the case of KP Zoo Limited, we demonstrated an understanding that these methods should be performed on selected items in order to have a better knowledge about how the business is running. Thus, the art of doing pure mathematics (i.e., ratio analysis) on the operating results and reading the chairman's statement, the auditor's report, and the notes to a financial statement can lead us to concrete evidence supported by the two equations theory (i.e., knowing the changes in a listed company's components such as, assets, liabilities, owner's equity, and cash flows—the driving forces affecting the earnings of a listed company).

Further to this discussion and analysis is an extra note intended to illustrate some pitfalls: Looking at the good results in an earnings announcement.

In an annual earnings announcement for any listed company, you may read a statement by management to show off its annual results. Some of the usual clauses used include the following:

- "We have made a great step in our *improvement on net assets* position to . . . a growth in 12.34 percent as compared to last year."
- "Our company remains strong, as we maintain over $12 million in *cash balances.*"
- "Our core business has had good results and *total comprehensive income* is reaching a high record. Our comprehensive income

contributable to ordinary shareholders is approximately stated at $123 million."

- "Despite keen competition, our group made a remarkable *gross profit* of $123.4 million as compared to the industrial average of approximately $98.76 million."

These are sample quotes for illustrative purposes only and show how there is sometimes a window dressing on the earnings and results of any listed company. This window dressing can be done in four main ways.

1. Purchase an Intangible Asset

The *improvement on net assets* window dressing can be done the following way:

The purchase cost of an intangible asset is very subjective and a lot of assumptions are used to derive the so-called fair value. Whenever the terms subjective and assumptions are used, room for manipulation of the true, fair value of intangible assets may arise, so that the valuation of overpriced intangible assets has a positive impact both on the earnings and the net assets position. However, if an economic downturn is expected in the next financial year ending, the result will be vice versa.

To take precaution, you can read the section on intangible assets in the notes to the financial statements. When doing so, consider the following questions:

- What are the intangible assets?
- How is the valuation of fair value done?
- What is the relevance of such for doing the business currently?
- What is the subsequent amortization expense of the intangible assets going to be on next year's income statement?

2. Borrowing a Short-Term Loan for One or Two Days Before the End of a Financial Period

The *cash balances* window dressing can be done in the following way:

A short-term loan may lead to a temporary rise of cash balances at the end of a financial year. However, the current liability is also increased at the same time. Under the cash flow concept, this eventually leads to a false position that the company has performed well in order to maintain favorable cash balances for the year.

To capture this, look in the section on financing activities in the statement of cash flows to determine whether a huge borrowing has been obtained. If you find one, ignore it during your overall consideration of the earnings announcement.

3. Various Gain/Translating Gains on Overseas Subsidiary Companies

The *total comprehensive income* window dressing can be done in the following way:

During ordinary business, the listed company may invest in available-for-sale investments (i.e., equity interests or debentures acquired) in order to enhance their earnings in a short-term period or invest in overseas subsidiary companies to keep its competitive strength globally.

Readers should look in the section on statement of comprehensive income to distinguish these positive income effects. During boom periods in stock markets, the positive upward adjustments on the market value of available-for-sale investments enhance growth in earnings. Further, the positive realignments on the exchange rate of overseas subsidiary companies makes additional recognized gains in the net assets of the overseas subsidiary companies.

4. Transactions with a Related Party

The *gross profit* window dressing can be done in the following way:

Sales/purchases of trade goods from a related party may cause a variation in the gross profits by manipulating the transfer pricing on such transactions. For instance, the underpriced purchases from a related party may lead to additional growth in a listed company's gross profits. On the other hand, the related party may trade at a loss position by selling undervalued goods to a listed company

To capture this, read the section in the notes of financial statements on related party transactions. Try to compare transactions in the same field in order to determine the commercial viability of such transactions.

SUMMARY

The discussions in this Appendix offer methods for readers to try and pinpoint the factors (pitfalls) that should be carefully considered to understand how data offered from a listed company can affect its earnings.

Readers should always try to determine the real drivers causing positive contributions in earnings. Digging down into the relevant sections of a listed company's annual report should be used to isolate the pitfalls, as addressed in the statement made by the management of the listed company. In return, readers will get a more concrete understanding of the earnings announcement without getting confused by false information.

About the Author

Alan Voon is the chief executive officer of Von Capital Limited and its associates at Warrants Capital Group, which are involved in asset management and capital market consultancy services. He is also the investment committee co-chairman of Huatai Von Malaysia Fund Segregated Portfolio, a Cayman Islands fund established by Huatai Financial Holdings (Hong Kong) Limited. Huatai Financial Holdings is a wholly owned subsidiary of Huatai Securities Company Limited, one of the largest stock brokers in mainland China and is listed on the Shanghai Stock Exchange. Huatai Von Malaysia Fund invests primarily in securities with a Malaysian theme throughout the world.

Mr. Voon hails from Kuala Lumpur, Malaysia and is considered an expert in Malaysia's warrants and derivatives market. He is the author of *Make Money Investing in Warrants on Bursa Malaysia* and *Money in Warrants*, the only books written on warrants in Malaysia thus far. He also conducts training and seminars in equity derivatives such as warrants and options.

Mr. Voon graduated from the DeGroote School of Business at McMaster University, Canada, in 1993 with a Master of Business Administration degree, majoring in Finance. Before that he completed an Honors Degree in Commerce, majoring in Accounting, at the same university.

Mr. Voon is a contributor to major newspapers and magazines in Malaysia such as the *Star, Nanyang SiangPao, China Press, Malaysia Business*, writing on topics related to derivatives, such as warrants, convertibles, options, and so on. His articles are also featured in www.warrants .com.my, a local warrants website run by Warrants Capital Group. He is also a sought-after speaker and consultant in the area of his expertise. His clients include international warrants issuers and listed companies.

In recent years, Mr. Voon has expanded his investment research into securities in the Greater China region and also into American Depository Receipts (ADRs). Through hard work and as a labor of love, he has quickly established a name in the international arena and has been invited to speak at various international investment fairs and conferences.

Index

Printed and bound by CPI Group (UK) Ltd, Croydon, CR0 4YY